THE
# TOP 100
# LOW-SALT
## RECIPES

THE
# TOP 100
# LOW-SALT
# RECIPES

Christine Bailey

## CONTROL YOUR BLOOD PRESSURE
## REDUCE YOUR RISK OF HEART DISEASE AND STROKE

## DUNCAN BAIRD PUBLISHERS
### LONDON

**The Top 100 Low-Salt Recipes**
Christine Bailey

Distributed in the USA and Canada by
Sterling Publishing Co., Inc.
387 Park Avenue South
New York, NY 10016-8810

This edition first published in the UK and USA in 2009 by
Duncan Baird Publishers Ltd
Sixth Floor, Castle House
75–76 Wells Street
London W1T 3QH

Managing Editor: Grace Cheetham
Editor: Nicole Bator
Managing Designer: Daniel Sturges
Designer: Sue Bush
Commissioned photography: Simon Scott
Food stylist: Mari Mererid Williams
Prop stylist: Helen Trent

Library of Congress Cataloging-in-Publication Data available

ISBN: 978-1-84483-734-2

10 9 8 7 6 5 4 3 2 1

Typeset in Helvetica Condensed
Color reproduction by Colourscan, Singapore
Printed in China by Imago

I would like to thank everyone at Duncan
Baird Publishers, especially Grace, for their
ongoing help and advice with this book
during its production. My thanks also to my
wonderful husband Chris and our children
Nathan, Isaac and Simeon for their endless
support, encouragement and tireless taste-
testing of all the recipes.

**Publisher's Note**
The information in this book is not intended as a substitute for
professional medical advice and treatment. If you are pregnant
or breastfeeding or have any special dietary requirements or
medical conditions, it is recommended that you consult a
medical professional before following any of the information
or recipes contained in this book. Duncan Baird Publishers,
or any other persons who have been involved in working on
this publication, cannot accept responsibility for any errors
or omissions, inadvertent or not, that may be found in the
recipes or text, or for any problems that may arise as a result
of preparing one of these recipes or following the advice
contained in this work.

**Notes on the Recipes**
Unless otherwise stated:
Use large eggs, and medium fruit and vegetables
Use unsalted butter and fresh ingredients, including herbs
Flours should be spooned into a measuring cup.
1 tsp = 5ml   1 tbsp = 15ml   1 cup = 240ml

Symbols are used to identify even small amounts of an
ingredient, such as the seeds symbol for sunflower oil. Dairy
foods in this book may include cow, goat, or sheep milk. The
vegetarian symbol is given to recipes using cheese; please
check the manufacturer's labelling before purchase to ensure
cheeses are vegetarian. Check that only the relevantly identified
foods are given to anyone with a food allergy or intolerance.

For information about custom editions, special sales,
and premium and corporate purchases, please contact
Sterling Special Sales Department at 800-805-5489
or specialsales@sterlingpub.com.

# contents

# KEY TO SYMBOLS

**V Suitable for vegetarians:** These dishes do not contain any meat, fish, or poultry. Often high in potassium, they can improve mineral balance and lower blood pressure. Check labels to ensure all cheeses are suitable for vegetarians.

**Contains dairy:** Dairy allergies can cause asthmalike symptoms, abdominal pains, and eczema. Try low-salt alternatives, such as fortified soymilk, yogurts, cheeses, and rice, oat, or nut milk. Use coconut or olive oil instead of butter.

**Contains eggs:** Use 1 to 2oz. tofu mashed with a little water, or 1 tbsp. arrowroot mixed with 3 tbsp. water for each egg; or use a commercial egg replacer.

**Contains gluten:** Intolerance to gluten, a protein in wheat, rye, barley, and oats, can cause inflammation, digestive problems, and other ailments. Gluten-free grains include buckwheat, millet, rice, quinoa, and corn.

**Contains nuts:** Substitute different unsalted seeds for nuts, if necessary.

**Contains seeds:** If necessary, omit seeds or use dried fruit or oats in baking instead. Replace seed oils with olive oil.

**Contains sugar:** Agave, fructose, and xylitol sweeten without raising blood sugar levels in the same way as regular sugar.

**Contains wheat:** Alternatives include corn, buckwheat, rice, quinoa, barley, rye, and millet. Gluten-free flour mixes and wheat-free breads are available—check salt levels as they vary between brands.

# INTRODUCTION

Enjoying great, healthy, homecooked food with family and friends is one of life's greatest pleasures. But in our fast-paced world, it can seem easier to microwave a frozen meal or phone for takeout than to cook a wholesome meal from scratch. With so many processed and time-saving food products available, it is tempting to throw a jar, package, or can in your shopping cart instead of heading to the fresh produce aisle. And all too often in this fast-food world, our diets fall short. Rather than nourishing our bodies, the foods we eat are actually damaging our health. This is particularly true when it comes to the amount of sodium we consume from salt in our diets. We are becoming increasingly aware of the need to watch our salt intake—and for good reason. Eating too much salt can raise blood pressure, increase the risk of heart disease and stroke, and lead to other health problems, such as certain cancers, kidney disease, and osteoporosis. Yet, it is estimated that the average American eats 50 percent too much salt. The American Heart Association says healthy adults should not eat more than 2,300 milligrams sodium a day, which is about one teaspoon salt.

For many people, reducing their salt intake equates to bland food or spending hours in the kitchen preparing complicated meals. But with a little savvy shopping and the help of the 100 recipes in this book, you will discover how flavorful low-salt cooking can be.

## ABOUT THIS BOOK

This book aims to inspire you to cook recipes that are low in salt and full of nutritious ingredients. It will show you how to use flavorings, herbs, and spices as alternatives to salt to create healthy, tantalizing meals you can enjoy every day. Whether cooking for one, feeding a family, or entertaining friends on a special occasion, you will find an irresistible selection of ideas for delicious breakfasts, lunches, side dishes, afternoon snacks, dinners, and desserts. Many of the recipes are quick and easy to prepare, while others can be assembled in advance to take the hassle out of mealtimes.

All the recipes have been created to make the most of the flavors that wholesome, fresh, good-quality ingredients offer—so there's no compromising on taste. You will find inspiration from around the world to give bold, fresh flavors to your food: lemongrass, lime, and gingerroot from Asia; pomegranate molasses from the Middle East; and fiery chilies, paprika, and peppers from South America.

Many people follow a low-salt diet to keep their blood pressure down or to improve their overall health and energy levels. These recipes, therefore, are based around superfoods, such as fresh fruits and vegetables, heart-healthy oils, and lean fish and meat, to provide plenty of essential nutrients, while also being low in saturated fats and sugars.

These recipes do not contain any added salt. Occasionally, ingredients are used that have some added salt, such as bread or tortillas, but each recipe contains less than 350mg salt (140mg sodium) per serving. Read food labels carefully to find the best low-salt versions of ingredients that do contain salt.

## WHAT IS SALT?

Salt is the common name for sodium

chloride, and it is the sodium that is most damaging to health. Sodium is needed by the body in small amounts to help maintain the right balance of fluids, to assist in transmitting nerve impulses, and to aid the contraction and relaxation of muscles. The kidneys help regulate the amount of sodium in the body— when levels are high, excess sodium is excreted in the urine. When sodium intake becomes too high, the kidneys aren't able to eliminate all of the excess and it starts to accumulate in the blood. This leads to excess fluid retention and increased blood pressure and can result in a number of health problems.

## SALT AND HEALTH

There is now strong evidence to suggest that a high intake of salt can lead to high blood pressure and damage your heart. Salt makes our bodies retain water, and if we eat too much salt, our bodies hold onto too much water. The extra fluid retained by the body leads to an increase in the pressure in our blood—resulting in high blood pressure (hypertension).

This can cause long-term health problems. In fact, people with high blood pressure are three times more likely to develop heart disease and stroke. These are the No. 1 and No. 3 killers in the United States today. It is estimated that reducing salt intake by 6,000mg a day, coupled with a healthier lifestyle, could reduce the risk of heart attacks worldwide by 18 percent and strokes by 24 percent. This equates to preventing approximately 2.6 million deaths each year. A high salt intake can also lead to other health problems, including a greater risk of certain cancers, kidney disease, obesity, fluid retention, and asthma attacks; and to an increase in calcium excreted in the urine, which can contribute to osteoporosis and significantly raise the risk of fractures.

And it's not just adults who are affected. Children are also consuming far too much salt, which can increase the risk of developing diseases later in life. The American Heart Association recommends that children aged one to three consume less than 1,500mg sodium a day; ages four to three, less than 1,900mg; nine to thirteen, less than 2,200mg; 14 to 18, less than 2,300mg. Tempting and convenient as they are, the abundance of convience foods, takeout, packaged processed foods, and snack foods, such as potato chips, cookies, and carbonated drinks, all contribute significantly to high-salt diets.

Don't be fooled into thinking other forms of salt are any healthier—kosher salt and sea salt are no different from ordinary table salt. Flavored salts, such as garlic, onion, and celery salts, should also be avoided. Several reduced-sodium salts are now widely available; these taste a little different from traditional sea salt and contain a high percentage of potassium. If you have heart or kidney problems, you should consult your doctor before using these products because of their potassium chloride levels.

Many people mistakenly believe that we need more salt during hot weather or strenuous exercise because a lot is lost through increased perspiration. In fact, it is water that needs to be replaced. The body is able to make adjustments and can easily survive on just 1,000mg salt per day. Muscle cramps are normally a sign of dehydration rather than a lack of salt, so remember to drink plenty of water, especially on hot days or before, during, and after exercise.

## MAIN SOURCES OF SALT

Fast food, takeout, restaurant meals, and cafeteria lunches can be very high in salt, but 80 percent of the salt in our diets comes from processed and packaged foods that we use at home. Staples, such as breads,

# HIGH-SALT FOODS

The following foods are often high in salt/sodium. Check food labels because brands can vary. Look out for low-salt versions of your favorites.

## Bakery and Grains

Breads, especially flavored breads, pitas, bagels, brioche; breadcrumbs

Breakfast cereals

Crackers and cookies

Pastries, such as croissants, Danishes, apple turnovers

Commercial desserts and cakes, cheesecakes, pies, fruit tarts, muffins

Batter, coating, pancake and cake mixes

## Dairy

Hard and semihard cheeses, such as cheddar, Parmesan, pecorino, Gouda, Edam, havarti, Jarlsberg, halloumi, feta, and smoked cheeses

Soft cheeses, such as cottage cheese (especially flavored varieties), and cheese spreads

Salted butters and spreads

## Canned Foods

Beans and lentils in salted water

Baked beans

Olives and capers

Fish or vegetables in brine

Soups

Cooking sauces

Canned spaghetti

## Meat, Fish, and Seafood

Sausages,

Salami, smoked meats, bacon, corned beef

Ham, especially prosciutto

Smoked fish, such as mackerel fillets, smoked salmon, and trout

Prepared fish dishes, such as fishcakes and fish sticks

Fish pastes and pâtés; spreads, such as taramasalata; anchovies

## Condiments

Soy sauce, teriyaki sauce, barbecue sauce, miso, ketchup, tomato paste, mustard, mayonnaise, pickles, salad dressings

Gravy mixes, bouillon cubes and powders, yeast extracts

Seasoned salts, such as celery, onion, and garlic salt

## Snack Foods and Beverages

Potato chips, cheesy and salted crackers, pretzels, salted nuts

Packaged sandwiches, fries, burgers, pizza, quiches

Prepared meals, such as pasta dishes; Chinese and Indian meals

Hot chocolate drinks; tomato and vegetable juices; many carbonated drinks

cheese, and breakfast cereals, as well as cooking sauces, soups, condiments like tomato ketchup and mayonnaise, and even store-bought puddings, cakes, and cookies can contribute a lot to our daily salt intake, especially if eaten on a daily basis. A typical teriyaki marinade, for example, can have up to 2,000mg salt per tablespoon (one third of the daily maximum recommended adult intake), and Dijon mustard can have 1,000mg per tablespoon.

## SWITCHING TO A LOW-SALT DIET

Changing to a low-salt diet doesn't have to mean your food will taste bland. In fact, too much salt can actually mask the flavor of food. As you start to reduce the amount of salt you use, you will begin to discover a whole new range of exciting flavors. It will also force you to cook more foods from scratch and focus on good-quality, fresh ingredients for flavor, which will also benefit your overall health. Adjust your salt

### SALT LEVELS—HIGH or LOW?

The percent daily values listed on the Nutrition Facts label on foods indicates how much a serving of that food contributes to your total daily nutrient intake. Values of 5 percent or less contain less than 140mg of sodium, so are considered low in sodium; 20 percent or more is considered high in sodium.

| Salt content | Amount of sodium per serving | Amount of salt per serving |
| --- | --- | --- |
| Sodium-free | Less than 5mg serving | less than 12.5mg |
| Very low sodium | 35mg or less per serving | less than 87.5mg |
| Low sodium | 145 mg or less per serving | less than 362.5mg |

intake gradually: it normally takes three to four weeks for your taste buds to adapt to less salt.

## READING FOOD LABELS

Food labels can be something of a minefield, especially when it comes to working out how much salt a product contains. Processed foods list the main ingredients in order of weight. Although salt is very light in weight and, therefore, can appear toward the end of an ingredients list, that product can still contain a hefty amount of salt, so always check the nutritional information, too.

Food labels often list the sodium content of the product rather than the salt (sodium chloride) content, so trying to keep track of how much salt you're eating can be confusing. One thousand milligrams of sodium is equivalent to 2,500mg salt, so to convert sodium to salt just multiply the sodium figure by 2.5. For example, potato chips often contain as much as 370mg sodium per ounce—or 925mg salt.

Look out for ingredients that contain the word "sodium," which means the food probably has a high sodium content. These ingredients can occur in a wide range of foods and include additives such as monosodium glutamate (a flavor enhancer), sodium nitrate (a preservative), sodium bicarbonate (a raising agent), and sodium saccharin (a sweetener).

## COOKING TECHNIQUES

Experiment with different cooking methods to help retain the natural flavors in the food. Stir-frying is a quick and simple way to cook vegetables, meat, and fish. Adding spices and herbs, fruit, wine, seasoned vinegars, and flavored oils can transform a familiar dish into a taste sensation. If you like soy sauce, try tamari instead. It is a wheat-free version that is often lower in salt than regular brands.

Pan-frying meat or fish before adding it to a dish and roasting, barbecuing, and broiling are all great ways to concentrate flavors and let the natural sugars in the food caramelize—creating a sweeter, richer taste. Use salt-free marinades and spice rubs—they not only add flavor, they keep the food moist while it cooks.

Steaming, another healthy and quick-cooking method, prevents vegetables from becoming too soggy and leaching out valuable nutrients and flavor. Fish is wonderful steamed—wrap it in lettuce leaves, grape leaves, or parchment paper to retain the juices. Or tuck in a few slices of lemon or lime, fresh herbs, or more-exotic spices to create exciting flavors.

## TOP TIPS FOR REDUCING SALT INTAKE

- Ditch the salt shaker. Keep it off the table and don't add salt before tasting food.
- Use fresh or frozen vegetables and fresh poultry, fish, and lean meat.
- Use less salt in cooking. You can reduce or even eliminate the salt from most recipes without affecting flavor.
- Avoid "instant" and "flavored" packaged and processed foods.
- Choose canned foods packed in water only. Avoid foods in brine or labeled as "cured," "smoked," or "pickled."
- Make your own healthy snacks, such as cinnamon-flavored popcorn, or snack on unsalted nuts and seeds.
- Replace high-salt processed breakfast cereals with rolled oats and homemade muesli and granola (see pages 27–9).
- Make your own stock (see page 18), or reserve the water when steaming vegetables and use it as a broth.
- Use olive oil, unsalted butter, or unsalted nut and seed butters for spreading.
- Make your own marinades, chili pastes, spice blends, and salad dressings.
- Use wine and fruit juices to add moisture and flavor.

- Eat more fruit and vegetables—they are rich in potassium, and they can help balance the sodium levels in your body.
- Flavor your food with fresh and dried herbs and spices.
- Read food labels, especially on staples like bread and cereals; sodium levels vary between brands, so choose wisely.

## HOW POTASSIUM CAN HELP

Reducing your sodium intake is only half the battle. Sodium is just one of several important mineral salts present in the body—others include potassium and magnesium. For optimum health, these minerals need to be in proper balance. Potassium and sodium are intricately related in the body and work together to maintain the correct water balance and proper nerve and muscle impulses. The more sodium you eat, the more potassium you need to keep the balance in check. Too much sodium coupled with too little

potassium can lead to cardiovascular disease, cancers, and water retention. The best sources of potassium are fruit and vegetables (see below).

### TOP POTASSIUM-RICH FOODS

Most fruit and vegetables are rich in potassium, so aim to eat at least five, but ideally seven, portions a day. Here are some great choices:

- Asparagus
- Avocado
- Banana
- Celery
- Cucumber
- Dark green leafy vegetables, such as spinach, broccoli, Brussels sprouts, kale, chard
- Fennel
- Fresh or dried figs and apricots; prunes
- Honeydew melon
- Papaya
- Potato

# SMART SHOPPING

If preparing flavorful meals without the salt shaker sounds like a tall order, then forward planning and organization make it much easier. The first step is keeping a well-stocked kitchen. The following lists provide a useful starting point. There are lots of really good low-sodium ingredients here, as well as many healthy foods, herbs, and flavorings that are frequently used in the recipes in this book. Most of them can be found in supermarkets. If you can't find them, try your local natural foods store.

## Foods for Your Refrigerator

- Cheese: low-salt varieties—check labels, but good options include goat cheese, mozzarella, ricotta, Gruyère, Swiss cheese, cream cheese
- Eggs: preferably organic and enriched with omega-3
- Fresh fish, poultry, and lean meat
- Fresh fruit and vegetables
- Fresh herbs
- Fruit juices, such as orange and grape, for flavoring
- Milk: 2% or skim; or dairy-free alternatives, such as soy, nut, oat, or quinoa milk
- Nuts and seeds: unsalted; store in the refrigerator for freshness
- Nut and seed butters: unsalted; rich in healthy omega-3 and omega-6 fats
- Tofu (soybean curd): plain, firm, or silken—avoid smoked versions
- Yogurt: plain yogurt with live cultures, sheep or goat milk yogurt, soy yogurt

## Pantry Staples

- Brown basmati rice, whole-wheat pasta, egg noodles, buckwheat or soba noodles
- Canned coconut milk
- Canned fish in water or olive oil
- Dried herbs and spices
- Good-quality dark chocolate
- Harissa paste, low-salt tomato paste
- Honey, fructose, xylitol, and agave nectar
- Low-salt breads, pita bread, crackers, and tortillas (look for less than 140mg salt per slice); plain muffins and quick breads
- Marinated artichoke hearts in oil or water
- Mirin, tamari (wheat-free soy sauce), reduced-salt soy sauce
- Oats, rolled oats, low-salt oatcakes, rye and barley flakes, wheat bran
- Olive oil or coconut oil (for cooking); hempseed, flaxseed, or extra virgin olive oil (for dressings)
- Quinoa, millet, barley, buckwheat
- Roasted red peppers in oil
- Tahini (sesame seed paste)
- Vanilla extract, rose water
- Whole-wheat flour, buckwheat flour, rice flour, gluten-free flour mixes
- Wine and spirits (for cooking)

## THE RECIPES IN THIS BOOK

Olive oil is used for cooking in these recipes. A monounsaturated fat, it is less susceptible to damage from heat, which can transform oils into harmful trans fats. Another excellent cooking oil is coconut oil, which does not raise cholesterol or produce harmful trans fats when cooked.

Some recipes call for a little sugar or honey to sweeten them. Fructose is a natural sugar alternative that does not raise blood sugar levels in the same way as regular sugar does. It is also lower in calories. Xylitol and agave nectar are also excellent natural substitutes for regular sugar and they do not have such a negative effect on blood sugar levels. These are readily available in natural food stores and most supermarkets.

Whenever possible, choose fresh, seasonal food and opt to buy as much organic produce as your budget will allow—especially meat and dairy products.

Eating seasonally ensures your food is fresher, packed with vital nutrients, and full of natural flavor—all of which make it easier for you and the people you cook for to ditch the salt.

## SPECIAL DIETS

Each recipe comes with an explanation of its health benefits as well as some serving suggestions to enable you to create a nutritionally balanced meal or snack. They have been created to appeal to the whole family, making meal-planning easier and quicker. Many of the recipes are also suitable for particular diets. Whether you are a vegetarian or have an allergy or sensitivity to gluten, wheat, dairy products, eggs, nuts, seeds, or sugar, you will find a range of healthy and delicious recipes to suit your every need—without worrying about unwanted reactions. Check the easy-to-read symbols at the top of each recipe for immediate reference.

## GETTING AHEAD

For delicious low-salt meals in minutes, it's worth preparing a few simple basics in advance. These versatile staples can be made ahead of time; the stock, peppers, and tomato sauce can also be frozen.

## Asian-Style Vinaigrette

This aromatic dressing is delicious on salads or served with meat and fish.

*Makes about ½ cup*
*Preparation: 10 minutes*

1 garlic clove, chopped
1 red chili, seeded and chopped
1 lemongrass stalk, thinly sliced
1 tsp. chopped gingerroot
2 tbsp. Thai fish sauce
2 tbsp. honey
¼ cup lime juice
freshly ground black pepper

**1** Put all the ingredients in a blender, season with pepper, and blend briefly until smooth.

## Homemade Vegetable Stock

Vary the vegetables in this recipe according to what you have available and what's in season. Save the water used when steaming vegetables—it also makes a great basic stock.

*Makes 1 quart*
*Preparation + Cooking: 10 + 45 minutes*

1 onion, sliced
2 carrots, peeled and sliced
2 leeks, sliced
2 celery stalks with leaves, chopped
2 bay leaves
1 handful parsley sprigs
1 handful broccoli stems

**1** Put all the ingredients in a large saucepan and cover with boiling water. Return to a boil, then reduce the heat and simmer 30 to 45 minutes until tender.
**2** Strain the stock through a strainer and discard the vegetables. Let cool. Cover and chill in the refrigerator.

## Roasted Peppers

Sweet and full of flavor, roasted peppers are delicious and so simple to make. Add them to salads, wraps, and pasta or stir them into couscous. For variety and to add color, prepare green, yellow, and orange bell peppers the same way.

*Serves: 4*
*Preparation + Cooking: 5 + 15 minutes*

**4 red bell peppers, halved and seeded**

**1** Preheat the broiler to high. Put the peppers, cut-sides down, on a baking sheet and grill 15 minutes, or until the skins blacken.
**2** Transfer the peppers to a bowl, cover with plastic wrap, and let cool.
**3** Peel off and discard the skins.

## Tomato Sauce

This tangy sauce makes a great base for soups, stews, and pasta sauces.

*Serves: 4–6*
*Preparation + Cooking: 10 + 30 minutes*

**1 tbsp. olive oil**
**1 onion**
**2 garlic cloves**
**2 carrots, peeled and cut into chunks**
**1 butternut squash, peeled, seeded, and cut into chunks**
**14oz. canned plum tomatoes, no added salt**
**2 cups chopped tomatoes**
**1¼ cups Homemade Vegetable Stock (see page 18)**
**2 tbsp. chopped parsley**

**1** Heat the oil in a large saucepan. Add the onion and garlic and cook over medium heat 3 to 4 minutes until soft. Add the remaining ingredients. Bring to a boil, reduce the heat, and simmer 20 minutes, or until the vegetables are tender.
**2** Transfer the mixture to a blender and blend 2 to 3 minutes until smooth.

# BREAKFASTS

Some of the worst-offending high-salt foods include breakfast cereals, breads, and morning pastries—staples in many homes and especially popular with children. In this chapter, you'll find a mouthwatering selection of healthy homemade alternatives, such as tempting Vanilla & Spice Granola, delicious Blueberry Buttermilk Pancakes, and savory Oat Muffins with Eggs & Spinach. Discover how to use flavorful ingredients like tangy fruits and fruit juices, crunchy nuts and seeds, and a variety of fresh and dried herbs and spices to create amazing flavors without adding salt. Loaded with nutrients, these recipes also give you a great start to the day—and keep you alert and focused, without those midmorning energy slumps.

**SERVES 4**

**PREPARATION + COOKING**
10 + 4 minutes

**STORAGE**
Store the oat topping in an airtight container 3 to 4 weeks. The smoothie is best drunk immediately, but it will keep in the refrigerator 4 to 5 hours.

**SERVE THIS WITH...**
Baked Eggs with Harissa
(see page 38)

**HEALTH BENEFITS**
Bananas are rich in potassium, an important mineral for promoting healthy blood pressure. They also contain pectin, a fiber that helps relieve ulcers and inflammation in the digestive tract and lowers cholesterol.

# mango & oat smoothie

Smoothies are a great way to start the day. Simple to prepare, they can be whizzed up in minutes, using nutritious, flavorsome ingredients. The oat and nut topping on this smoothie will keep you energized all morning.

1 tbsp. olive oil
1 cup rolled oats
½ cup chopped hazelnuts
½ cup slivered almonds
1 tbsp. ground flaxseed

1 mango, peeled, seeded,
 and chopped
2 bananas, chopped
²/₃ cup plain yogurt
juice of ½ orange

**1** Heat the oil in a nonstick skillet. Add the oats and toast, stirring occasionally, 2 to 3 minutes until golden. Add the hazelnuts and almonds and toast 1 minute longer. Remove from the heat and let cool, then stir in the flaxseed.
**2** Put the mango, bananas, yogurt, and orange juice in a blender or food processor. Blend until smooth. Pour into glasses and top with the rolled oats. Serve with a spoon.

# pineapple, lime & avocado smoothie

This creamy smoothie is packed with heart-protecting nutrients. Avocados are rich in healthy monounsaturated fat, fiber, folic acid, iron, and vitamin E. They are also one of the top fruit sources of potassium, which is essential for healthy blood pressure and reducing fluid retention.

| | |
|---|---|
| 1 avocado, halved and pitted | 1 tsp. lime juice |
| 2 cups fresh pineapple juice | 2 tsp. honey |

**1** Remove the flesh from the avocado and place in a blender or food processor. Add the remaining ingredients and blend 1 to 2 minutes until smooth and creamy.
**2** Pour into glasses and serve immediately.

**SERVES 2**

**PREPARATION TIME**
5 minutes

**STORAGE**
Best drunk immediately.

**SERVE THIS WITH...**
Vanilla & Spice Granola
(see page 27)

**HEALTH BENEFITS**
Pineapple contains bromelain, an enzyme that aids digestion by helping to break down proteins. It possesses anti-inflammatory properties and can help reduce the stickiness of blood, making it useful for conditions such as angina and thrombosis. It is a useful diuretic, too, and can help balance body fluids.

# spicy tomato juice

**SERVES 4**

**PREPARATION**
10 minutes

**STORAGE**
Best drunk immediately, but
will keep in the refrigerator
up to 12 hours.

**SERVE THIS WITH…**
Oat Muffins with Eggs & Spinach
(see page 34)

**HEALTH BENEFITS**
Celery contains active
compounds called pthalides,
which relax the muscles of the
arteries that regulate blood
pressure. Both cucumber and
celery are powerful diuretics
and, being rich in potassium,
are useful for relieving water
retention and combating
excess sodium intake.

Many commercial drinks, including tomato
juice, contain surprisingly high levels of
salt and other additives. Making your own
guarantees they include nothing but fresh,
nutritious ingredients. This juice has plenty
of vitamin C and beta-carotene to help
support the immune system.

10 large ripe tomatoes, cut into
  chunks
1 red bell pepper, seeded and
  cut into chunks
3 celery stalks, roughly
  chopped

½ large cucumber, cut into
  sticks
1-in. piece gingerroot, peeled
crushed ice, to serve (optional)

**1** Push all the ingredients through a juicer.
**2** Serve in glasses over ice, if you like.

# cranberry & cherry compote

This delicious, salt-free compote is packed full of heart-protecting and immune-boosting antioxidants. Spoon it over pancakes or muesli or stir it into plain yogurt for a sweet treat.

| | |
|---|---|
| 1 cup dried cranberries | ¼ cup apple juice |
| 1 cup dried cherries | 1 cinnamon stick |
| ¾ cup dried apricots | 5 cloves |
| 2 apples, peeled, cored, and chopped | 2 tbsp. grated orange zest |

**1** Put the dried fruit in a bowl and cover with warm water. Let soak 15 minutes, then drain.

**2** Put the soaked fruit in a saucepan with the remaining ingredients. Bring to a boil, then reduce the heat and simmer 10 to 15 minutes, breaking up the fruit until the mixture thickens. Serve hot or at room temperature.

**SERVES 4**

**PREPARATION + COOKING**
5 + 15 minutes + soaking

**STORAGE**
Make in advance and keep in the refrigerator up to 5 days or freeze up to 1 month.

**SERVE THIS WITH...**
Lemon Buckwheat Blinis (see page 32)

**HEALTH BENEFITS**
Cranberries and cherries are rich in antioxidants, particularly vitamin C and flavonoids called anthocyanins, which support the body's immune system and protect against cancer and heart disease. They also work together to strengthen the veins and arteries, aiding circulation.

**PREPARATION + COOKING**
5 + 15 minutes

**STORAGE**
Make in advance and keep in the refrigerator up to 1 week.

**SERVE THIS WITH...**
Apricot & Almond Muesli
(see page 28)

**HEALTH BENEFITS**
Prunes are particularly high in antioxidants, which can help protect the body against cancers, heart disease, and aging. They also supply plenty of potassium, useful for lowering high blood pressure and eliminating excess sodium from the body.

# cardamom & fruit compote

This aromatic concoction is great on its own for breakfast or as a healthy dessert. Dried fruit is an excellent way to add flavor without adding salt. High in soluble fiber, it also boosts energy and can help lower cholesterol.

½ cup dried apricots
1½ cups dried pears or
    peaches, chopped
½ cup prunes, pitted
½ cup dried cherries
½ cup dried figs

1 tbsp. cardamom seeds,
    crushed
4 cloves
juice of 3 oranges
1 tbsp. orange-flower water

**1** Put all the ingredients in a heavy-bottomed saucepan. Add 1 cup water and bring to a boil. Reduce the heat and simmer 15 minutes, or until the fruit is tender.
**2** Serve warm or at room temperature.

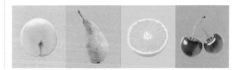

Ⓥ Ⓓ Ⓓ Ⓓ Ⓓ

# vanilla & spice granola

This delicious version of the breakfast favorite is full of nutritious, slow energy-releasing grains, plus antioxidant-rich berries. The nuts and seeds supply the body with plenty of protein and essential fats to keep you energized and focused until lunchtime.

**SERVES 4 TO 6**

**PREPARATION + COOKING**
10 + 20 minutes

**STORAGE**
Make in advance and store in an airtight container up to 1 month.

**SERVE THIS WITH...**
Cardamom & Fruit Compote (see page 26)
plain yogurt or milk

**HEALTH BENEFITS**
Although nuts are high in fat, it is predominantly healthy monounsaturated fat, which can protect against heart disease. Nuts are also rich in other heart-friendly nutrients, including vitamin E, folic acid, calcium, magnesium, and zinc.

2 cups rolled oats
1¼ cups barley flakes
½ cup slivered almonds
½ cup chopped walnuts
¼ cup pumpkin seeds
¼ cup sunflower seeds
3 tbsp. sesame seeds

5 tbsp. apple juice
5 tbsp. honey
3 tbsp. olive oil
2 tbsp. vanilla extract
1 tsp. ground cinnamon
½ tsp. ground nutmeg
¾ cup dried berries

**1** Preheat the oven to 350°F. Put the rolled oats, barley flakes, almonds, walnuts, and seeds in a large bowl and mix well. In a separate bowl, mix together the apple juice, honey, oil, vanilla extract, cinnamon, and nutmeg. Pour this mixture over the dry ingredients and stir well.

**2** Tip the mixture onto two baking sheets and spread out evenly. Bake 20 minutes, stirring occasionally, until golden. Remove from the oven and let cool. Mix in the dried berries and serve.

**HEALTH BENEFITS**
Oats and wheat germ are rich in slow-releasing carbohydrates to keep energy levels sustained right through the morning. They also contain a type of soluble fiber called beta-glucan, which is useful for balancing blood sugar levels and lowering cholesterol.

# *apricot & almond muesli

This nutrient-rich muesli is bursting with so much flavor, you won't miss the salt that is often added to store-bought versions. Toasting the rolled oats brings out its sweet nuttiness, and the dried apricots are a great source of iron.

olive oil, for greasing
2½ cups rolled oats
3 tbsp. wheat germ
2 tbsp. shredded unsweetened coconut flakes
1 tsp. ground cinnamon
½ cup chopped almonds
1 cup apple juice
½ cup chopped dried apricots

**SERVES 8**

**PREPARATION + COOKING**
10 + 25 minutes

**STORAGE**
Make in advance and store in an airtight container up to 4 weeks.

**SERVE THIS WITH...**
Cardamom & Fruit Compote (see page 26)
fresh fruit
plain yogurt, milk, nut milk, or coconut milk

**1** Preheat the oven to 350°F. Lightly grease three baking sheets with oil. Put the rolled oats, wheat germ, coconut, cinnamon, almonds, and apple juice in a large bowl and mix well.

**2** Spread the mixture out evenly on the baking sheets. Bake 25 minutes, stirring occasionally, until the muesli is evenly browned.

**3** Remove from the oven and let cool. Stir in the chopped apricots and serve.

Use millet or quinoa flakes to make this recipe suitable for anyone with a sensitivity to gluten.

# apple, cinnamon & raisin oatmeal

Oatmeal is a healthy way to start the day. Packed with soluble fibre, oats are excellent for improving digestion.

**SERVES 4**

**PREPARATION + COOKING**
5 + 10 minutes

**STORAGE**
Soak the oats in the refrigerator overnight to speed up cooking the following morning.

**SERVE THIS WITH...**
Pineapple, Lime & Avocado Smoothie (see page 23)
plain yogurt and toasted seeds
fresh or poached fruit

**HEALTH BENEFITS**
Cinnamon is a great natural sweetener and flavoring. It acts in a similar way to the hormone insulin by helping to balance blood sugar levels, making it a natural aid for diabetics.

heaped 1 cup steel-cut oats
2 apples, peeled, cored, and chopped

1 tsp. ground cinnamon
1¼ cups milk or soymilk
½ cup raisins

**1** Put the oats, apples, cinnamon, and milk in a saucepan over medium heat and bring to a boil. Reduce the heat to low and simmer, stirring occasionally, 4 to 5 minutes until the mixture thickens and the oats soften. Alternatively, put the ingredients in a microwavable bowl and heat, covered, on High 5 minutes, stirring halfway through.
**2** Spoon the oatmeal into bowls, sprinkle with the raisins, and serve immediately.

(V)

# millet hot cakes

These hearty cakes make a healthy, satisfying breakfast and are equally delicious as an afternoon treat. Serve hot with fresh or poached fruit, or drizzle maple syrup over the top if you are feeling really indulgent.

2 cups millet
2½ cups apple juice
1 cup raisins
1 tsp. ground cinnamon

1 tbsp. rice flour, plus extra
  for rolling
²/₃ cup silken tofu
1 tbsp. olive oil

**1** Put the millet and apple juice in a pan and bring to a boil. Reduce the heat and simmer gently 25 minutes. Add the raisins and cook 5 minutes longer.

**2** Tip the mixture into the bowl of a food processor and add the cinnamon, rice flour, and tofu. Process briefly to form a soft dough. Transfer the dough to a lightly floured countertop and roll out to about 1in. thick. Using a 2½in. round cookie cutter, cut out 12 cakes.

**3** Heat the oil in a large skillet. Add the cakes and fry, in batches, 5 minutes on each side until golden. Let cool slightly, then serve.

**SERVES 4**

**PREPARATION + COOKING**
10 + 55 minutes

**STORAGE**
Make in advance and keep in the refrigerator up to 3 days or freeze up to 1 month. Warm through in the oven before serving.

**SERVE THIS WITH...**
Cranberry & Cherry Compote
  (see page 25)
plain or soy yogurt

**HEALTH BENEFITS**
Millet is a nutritious, gluten-free grain and a good source of protein. Rich in calcium, magnesium, potassium, and B vitamins, it is a wonderful stress-busting food. It is also highly alkaline and full of fiber, so it can improve digestion and help lower cholesterol levels.

010

Ⓥ Ⓞ ⬬ ⊙

# lemon buckwheat blinis

These fabulous gluten-free blinis, flavored with fresh lemon, are simple and quick to prepare. Make them dairy-free by replacing the milk with soy- or rice milk.

**MAKES 10**

**PREPARATION + COOKING**
10 + 15 minutes

**STORAGE**
Make in advance and keep in the refrigerator up to 3 days or freeze up to 1 month. To reheat, preheat the oven to 375°F. Put the blinis on a baking sheet, cover with foil, and bake 5 minutes, or until hot.

**SERVE THIS WITH...**
Cranberry & Cherry Compote (see page 25)
natural or soy yogurt with fresh or poached fruit

**HEALTH BENEFITS**
Despite its name, buckwheat isn't a grain, but a fruit seed related to rhubarb. It contains all eight essential amino acids, making it a good source of protein. Rich in fiber and flavonoids, particularly rutin, it strengthens capillaries and helps detoxify the body.

¾ cup buckwheat flour
1 tsp. gluten-free baking
  powder
2 tsp. fructose
1 egg, separated

¾ cup milk
1 tbsp. lemon juice
1 tsp. grated lemon zest
1 tbsp. olive oil

**1** Put the buckwheat flour, baking powder, fructose, egg yolk, milk, and lemon juice and zest in a bowl. Using a hand-held blender, blend until a smooth batter forms.
**2** In a separate, clean bowl, whisk the egg white until stiff. Fold it into the batter.
**3** Heat the oil in a large skillet. Place five spoonfuls of the batter in the pan, spacing well apart, and cook 2 to 3 minutes on each side until golden. Remove the blinis from the pan and keep them warm while you cook the remaining batter. Serve warm.

# blueberry buttermilk pancakes

Processed pancake mixes can contain a lot of added salt. For the perfect leisurely breakfast, whip up a teetering stack of these thick, fluffy homemade pancakes instead.

¾ cup plus 2 tbsp. whole-wheat flour
¾ cup plus 2 tbsp. all-purpose flour
2 tsp. baking powder

1 tbsp. fructose
2 eggs, separated
1 cup buttermilk or plain yogurt
¾ cup blueberries
1 tbsp. olive oil

**1** Sift the flours, baking powder, and fructose into a large bowl. In a separate bowl, mix together the egg yolks and buttermilk, then add this mixture to the dry ingredients, stirring until the mixture forms a batter.
**2** In another, clean bowl, whisk the egg whites until stiff. Fold them and the blueberries into the batter.
**3** Heat the oil in a skillet. Place about five spoonfuls of the batter in the pan, spacing well apart, and cook 2 to 3 minutes on each side until golden. Remove the pancakes from the pan and keep them warm while you cook the remaining batter. Serve warm.

**MAKES 8 TO 12**

**PREPARATION + COOKING**
10 + 15 minutes

**STORAGE**
Make in advance and keep in the refrigerator up to 2 days or freeze up to 1 month. To reheat, preheat the oven to 375°F. Put the pancakes on a baking sheet, cover with foil, and bake 5 minutes, or until hot.

**SERVE THIS WITH...**
Spicy Tomato Juice
  (see page 24)
fresh or poached berries
plain yogurt and maple syrup

**HEALTH BENEFITS**
Blueberries are a rich source of vitamin C and anthocyanins, the natural chemicals that give fruit their intense color. These potent chemicals protect the body against the effects of aging, help strengthen blood capillaries, and improve circulation.

012

# oat muffins with eggs & spinach

**HEALTH BENEFITS**
A well-known source of iron, spinach also contains other important nutrients, including calcium, magnesium, and vitamin K for bone health. It is rich in vitamin C, which helps iron absorption, and in heart-friendly potassium, folic acid, and vitamin B6.

Poached eggs are a great comfort food. Teeming with protein, vitamins, and minerals, they are also a great source of fuel to start the day. Combined here with savory oat muffins and spinach, they make a perfect, energy-packed, low-salt breakfast.

olive oil, for greasing
1¼ cups self-rising flour
½ tsp. baking powder
heaped ½ cup rolled oats
1 tsp. thyme

2 eggs, beaten
²/₃ cup milk or soymilk
7oz. baby spinach leaves
4 poached eggs, to serve
freshly ground black pepper

SERVES 4

PREPARATION + COOKING
15 + 20 minutes

STORAGE
The muffins can be made in advance and kept in an airtight container up to 2 days or frozen up to 1 month.

SERVE THIS WITH...
Mushroom & Garlic Medley (see page 39)
Pineapple, Lime & Avocado Smoothie (see page 23)

Experiment with different fresh herbs, such as basil, sage, and oregano, to give the muffins a bit of variety.

**1** Preheat the oven to 425°F and grease four holes of a muffin pan. Sift the flour and baking powder into a bowl and stir in the rolled oats and thyme. Beat in the eggs and milk to form a batter.

**2** Spoon the batter into the pan and bake 15 minutes, or until golden brown. Leave in the pan 1 minute, then transfer to a wire rack to cool completely.

**3** Put the spinach in a large saucepan over medium heat and cook 2 to 3 minutes, stirring occasionally, until just wilted. Split the muffins in half and toast them.

**4** Top one half of each muffin with some of the spinach, followed by 1 poached egg. Sprinkle with black pepper and serve immediately.

# baked beans

**SERVES 4**

**PREPARATION + COOKING**
5 + 15 minutes

**STORAGE**
Make in advance and keep in the
refrigerator up to 3 days.

**SERVE THIS WITH...**
Mushroom & Garlic Medley
(see page 39)
Mediterranean Tortilla (see
page 37)

**HEALTH BENEFITS**
Navy beans provide plenty
of protein to help maintain
energy levels and fiber, which
is important for lowering blood
cholesterol and improving
digestion. They are also rich in
B vitamins, which help combat
stress and lower homocysteine
levels—a high amount of which
can increase risk of heart disease.

This homemade recipe is much healthier than
the canned versions, which can be very high
in salt, sugar, and sweeteners. Use tamari,
a wheat-free, low-salt soy sauce, rather than
regular salty brands.

1 recipe quantity Tomato Sauce
   (see page 19)
15oz. canned navy beans, no
   added salt or sugar, drained
   and rinsed
a pinch allspice
a pinch ground cinnamon
3 tbsp. apple juice
2 tsp. tamari
1 tsp. cider vinegar
Oat Muffins (see page 34)
   or toast, to serve

**1** Put all the ingredients in a saucepan and bring to a boil.
Reduce the heat and simmer gently 15 minutes, or until
slightly thickened.
**2** Serve with oat muffins or toast.

Ⓥ Ⓞ

# mediterranean tortilla

This thick, Spanish-style omelet makes a hearty, protein-rich breakfast. It is also delicious cold, cut into wedges for packed lunches or picnics.

1 tbsp. olive oil
1 small sweet potato, peeled and cut into small cubes
1 red onion, finely chopped
1 red bell pepper, seeded and chopped

1 garlic clove, crushed
4 button mushrooms, sliced
1 handful basil, chopped
1 handful parsley, chopped
6 eggs, beaten
freshly ground black pepper

**1** Heat the oil in an ovenproof skillet with a flameproof handle. Add the potato and onion and cook 5 to 6 minutes, stirring occasionally, until the onion is soft. Add the bell pepper, garlic, and mushrooms and cook 5 minutes longer.

**2** Preheat the broiler to high. Stir the basil and parsley into the eggs and season to taste with black pepper. Pour the mixture over the vegetables in the pan, then reduce the heat, and cook gently 5 to 7 minutes until the eggs have almost set.

**3** Place the pan under the broiler and broil 3 to 4 minutes until the top of the tortilla is golden brown. Cut into wedges and serve.

**SERVES 4**

**PREPARATION + COOKING**
10 + 25 minutes

**STORAGE**
Make in advance and keep in the refrigerator up to 2 days.

**SERVE THIS WITH...**
Mango & Oat Smoothie (see page 22)
broiled tomatoes or Baked Beans (see page 36)

**HEALTH BENEFITS**
An excellent source of protein and easily digestible, eggs are rich in the immune-boosting nutrients iron, zinc, and selenium, as well as B vitamins for energy. Despite their image as a high-cholesterol food, eggs actually contain mostly monounsaturated fats, which help lower the risk of heart disease.

015

**V O**

# baked eggs
# with harissa

This luxurious breakfast treat is packed with
antioxidants, making it incredibly nutritious.

SERVES 4

PREPARATION + COOKING
10 + 35 minutes

STORAGE
Make the tomato mixture
in advance and keep in the
refrigerator up to 2 days.

SERVE THIS WITH...
Pumpkin & Seed Bread
 (see page 79)
Pineapple, Lime & Avocado
 Smoothie (see page 23)

HEALTH BENEFITS
Chilis are potent immune-system
boosters and effective natural
painkillers—even in small
quantities. They are also rich in
beta-carotene—the antioxidant
responsible for healthy skin and
eyes—and the phytochemical
capsaicin, which has natural
analgesic properties that can
help ease headaches, arthritis
and sinusitis.

1 tbsp. olive oil, plus extra
 for greasing
½ red onion, chopped
½ red bell pepper, seeded
 and chopped
½ yellow bell pepper, seeded
 and chopped
1 garlic clove, crushed
1 red chile, seeded and finely
 chopped
4 plum tomatoes, chopped
1 tsp. harissa
4 eggs
1 tbsp. chopped chives

**1** Preheat the oven to 375ºF and grease four ramekins.
Heat the oil in a skillet. Add the onion and peppers and
cook over low heat 2 to 3 minutes until soft. Add the
garlic, chile, tomatoes, and harissa and simmer 10 to 15
minutes until the sauce is thick.
**2** Spoon the mixture into the ramekins and make a slight
depression on the top of the mixtures. Break an egg into
each ramekin. Put the ramekins in a roasting pan and
pour in enough hot water to come halfway up the sides
of the ramekins.
**3** Bake 15 to 17 minutes until light brown on top. Sprinkle
with the chives and serve.

(V)

# mushroom & garlic medley

A fantastic flavoring to use instead of salt, garlic is a health-boosting superfood. It helps lower the body's levels of "bad" cholesterol while boosting the "good" cholesterol.

2 tbsp. olive oil
2 garlic cloves, crushed
2 shallots, finely chopped

9oz. mixed mushrooms, such as shiitake, cremini, portabellini, and oyster, thickly sliced
2 tbsp. chopped parsley
hot toast, to serve

**1** Heat the oil in a large skillet. Add the garlic and shallots and stir over medium heat 1 to 2 minutes until soft.
**2** Sprinkle with the parsley and serve on toast.

**SERVES 4**

**PREPARATION + COOKING**
5 + 8 minutes

**STORAGE**
Make in advance and keep in the refrigerator up to 3 days.

**SERVE THIS WITH...**
Oat Muffins with Eggs & Spinach (see page 34)
Baked Beans (see page 36)
Pineapple, Lime & Avocado Smoothie (see page 23)

**HEALTH BENEFITS**
Mushrooms are a good source of B vitamins and the mineral selenium—an important antioxidant that supports immune function. Shiitake mushrooms contain active components like lentinan, a polysaccharide compound that helps lower cholesterol and fight cancer.

# LUNCHES & SIDE DISHES

Ready-made and fast-food lunches, such as sandwiches, dips, pâtés, and soups, are notoriously high in salt, so making your own is one of the best ways to reduce your intake. By concentrating on the natural flavors of other ingredients—such as refreshing citrus, pungent sun-dried tomatoes, subtly bitter greens, and fiery chilies—you can create delicious low-salt dishes that will quickly become favorites. From simple lunches to more leisurely meals, the recipes in this chapter are full of delicious ideas, such as Pesto-Tuna Wraps and Thai-Style Seared Beef & Spinach Salad, that will keep you sustained all afternoon.

# roasted red pepper hummus

Homemade hummus is a breeze to make. This delicious version is packed with fiber, heart-healthy essential fatty acids, and antioxidants—without the salt and saturated fat found in many commercial dips.

**SERVES 4**

**PREPARATION**
10 minutes

**STORAGE**
Make in advance and keep in the refrigerator up to 1 week or freeze up to 1 month.

**SERVE THIS WITH...**
Sun-Dried Tomato Bread
(see page 80)
vegetable sticks, such as bell pepper, cucumber, and carrot; snow peas and baby corn
Cherry & Ricotta Tarts
(see page 132)

**HEALTH BENEFITS**
Chickpeas are an excellent source of protein and soluble fiber, which helps balance blood sugar levels and lower cholesterol. They contain fructo-oligosaccharides, a type of fiber that helps support friendly bacteria in the gut, important for a healthy digestive system.

1 large Roasted Pepper
(see page 19)
15oz. canned chickpeas, no added salt or sugar, drained and rinsed

1 tbsp. lemon juice
2 garlic cloves, crushed
1 tbsp. tahini
2 tbsp. flaxseed or hemp oil
a pinch paprika

**1** Put the pepper, chickpeas, lemon juice, garlic, and tahini in a food processor or blender. Blend 3 to 4 minutes until the mixture forms a thick puree. Add the oil and process 3 to 4 minutes longer until smooth and creamy.
**2** Spoon the hummus into a bowl, sprinkle with the paprika, and serve.

# sun-dried tomato dip

Sun-dried tomatoes give this dip a rich flavor without relying on processed salty sauces or pastes. Silken tofu is a great way to boost your intake of soy protein, which helps lower harmful cholesterol levels.

scant ½ cup sun-dried tomatoes
2 tsp. low-salt sun-dried
    tomato paste
9oz. silken tofu
1 garlic clove, crushed

1 tbsp. apple cider vinegar
1 tomato, seeded and chopped
a few drops Tabasco sauce
a pinch cayenne pepper

**1** Soak the sun-dried tomatoes in boiling water 15 minutes, then drain and roughly chop them. Put them in a food processor with the tomato paste, tofu, garlic, vinegar, and tomato. Blend 3 to 4 minutes until smooth, then season to taste with the Tabasco sauce.
**2** Spoon the dip into a bowl, sprinkle with the cayenne pepper, and serve.

**SERVES 4**

**PREPARATION**
10 minutes + soaking

**STORAGE**
Make in advance and keep in the refrigerator up to 4 days.

**SERVE THIS WITH...**
Spicy Tortilla Chips (see page 78) or plain oat crackers
vegetable sticks, such as carrot, bell pepper, cucumber, and celery
fresh fruit
Apple Crunch Cake (see page 85)

**HEALTH BENEFITS**
Tofu is rich in protein and B vitamins, low in saturated fat and sodium, and an important nondairy source of calcium. Soy protein is great for the heart as it can lower cholesterol and triglyceride levels and reduce the likelihood of blood clots forming.

# butternut squash & pear soup

This soup combines antioxidant-rich vegetables with juicy pears. Full of antiviral and antibacterial properties, it is perfect for boosting your protection against infection.

**SERVES 4**

**PREPARATION + COOKING**
15 + 35 minutes

**STORAGE**
Make in advance and keep in the refrigerator up to 3 days or freeze up to 1 month.

**SERVE THIS WITH...**
Sun-Dried Tomato Bread
  (see page 80)
low-salt cheese or lean turkey
Chocolate & Orange Soufflés
  (see page 133)
fresh fruit

**HEALTH BENEFITS**
Winter squashes and sweet potatoes are full of cancer-fighting, cardio-protective nutrients. They are rich in carotenoids and vitamins C and E—valuable antioxidants for skin, eyes, lungs, and immune system. A great source of soluble fiber, they can help lower cholesterol and aid diestion.

2 tbsp. olive oil
1 onion, chopped
2 cups peeled, seeded, and
    chopped butternut squash
1 sweet potato, peeled and
    chopped
3 pears, peeled, cored,
    and chopped

¼ tsp. garam masala
¼ tsp. cayenne pepper
2 cups Homemade Vegetable
    Stock (see page 18)
5 tbsp. crème fraîche
freshly ground black pepper

**1** Heat the oil in a large saucepan. Add the onion and cook over low heat 3 to 4 minutes until soft.
**2** Add the squash, potato, pears, spices, and stock to the pan. Bring to a boil, then reduce the heat and simmer 25 minutes, or until the squash is tender.
**3** Pour the soup into a food processor or blender and blend, in batches if necessary, until smooth. Return the soup to the rinsed pan, stir in the crème fraîche and season with black pepper. Heat through gently and serve.

# roasted garlic & tomato soup

Roasting the garlic and tomatoes lends this soup a rich, sweet flavor, and the beans and seeds provide valuable protein.

1 garlic bulb, cloves separated
  and peeled
2 tbsp. olive oil
1lb. tomatoes, quartered
15oz. canned borlotti beans, no
  added salt or sugar, drained
  and rinsed

$3^2/_3$ cups Homemade Vegetable
  Stock (see page 18)
1 tbsp. lemon juice
1 tbsp. chopped basil
2 tbsp. pumpkin seeds, toasted
2 tbsp. sunflower seeds,
  toasted

**1** Preheat the oven to 400°F. Put the garlic in a roasting pan, drizzle with the oil, and roast 15 minutes, or until brown. Add the tomatoes to the garlic and cook 10 to 15 minutes longer until the tomatoes are soft.
**2** Tip the tomatoes and garlic into a blender. Add the beans and stock and blend 2 to 3 minutes until smooth.
**3** Pour the soup into a saucepan and stir in the lemon juice and basil. Reheat over low heat, then ladle into bowls. Sprinkle with the seeds and serve immediately.

SERVES 4

PREPARATION + COOKING
10 + 35 minutes

STORAGE
Toast the seeds in advance and keep in an airtight container in the refrigerator up to 1 week. Make the soup in advance and keep in the refrigerator up to 3 days or freeze up to 1 month.

SERVE THIS WITH...
Chili-Corn Muffins
  (see page 83)
Date & Lemon Oat Bars
  (see page 89)
fresh fruit and plain yogurt

HEALTH BENEFITS
Tomatoes are rich in lycopene, a natural plant compound that is best absorbed by the body when tomatoes are cooked. Lycopene has been shown to protect against cancer and guard the skin and eyes from sun damage.

# pea & lettuce soup

Lettuce contains a compound that relaxes the nervous system and relieves stress.

**SERVES 4**

**PREPARATION + COOKING**
5 + 25 minutes

**STORAGE**
Make in advance and keep in the refrigerator up to 4 days or freeze up to 1 month.

**SERVE THIS WITH...**
Sesame Crackers (see page 76)
Pesto-Tuna Wraps (see page 48)
Summer Berry Crisp
 (see page 134)

**HEALTH BENEFITS**
Peas are a great heart-protecting food. Rich in folic acid and B vitamins, they can help lower homocysteine levels, a high level of which has been linked to heart disease. They also provide plenty of vitamin K, important for bone health and blood clotting.

1 tbsp. olive oil
1 onion, finely chopped
1 celery stalk
2¼ cups frozen shelled peas
2 hearts of lettuce, roughly
 chopped

3¼ cups Homemade Vegetable
 Stock (see page 18)
juice of ½ lemon
1 tbsp. chopped parsley
freshly ground black pepper

**1** Heat the oil in a saucepan. Add the onion and celery and cook over low heat 5 minutes, or until tender.

**2** Add the peas, lettuces, and stock. Bring to a boil, reduce the heat and simmer 15 minutes until the peas are tender. Stir in the lemon juice and season with black pepper.

**3** Pour the soup into a food processor or blender. Add the parsley and blend, in batches if necessary, until smooth. Return the soup to the rinsed pan, reheat over a low heat, and serve hot.

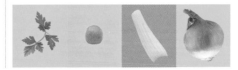

# chilled pepper & bean soup with basil cream

This crimson-colored soup is full of summer flavors and packed with healthy antioxidants.

1 tbsp. olive oil
1 onion, finely chopped
1 garlic clove, crushed
2½ cups Homemade Vegetable
   Stock (see page 18)
a pinch cayenne pepper

3 Roasted Peppers
   (see page 19), chopped
15oz. canned cannellini beans,
   no added salt or sugar,
   drained and rinsed
1 handful basil
6 tbsp. Greek yogurt

**1** Heat the oil in a large saucepan. Add the onion and garlic and cook over low heat 5 minutes, then add the stock, cayenne, bell peppers, and beans. Bring to a boil, then reduce the heat and simmer, covered, 15 to 20 minutes until the vegetables are tender.
**2** Pour the soup into a food processor or blender and blend, in batches, until smooth. Place a strainer over a large bowl and strain the soup, using a wooden spoon to push it through the strainer. Cover and chill 1 hour.
**3** Put the basil and yogurt in a blender and blend for 1 minute until combined. Serve the chilled soup drizzled with the basil cream.

SERVES 4

PREPARATION + COOKING
10 + 25 minutes + chilling

STORAGE
Make the soup in advance and keep in the refrigerator up to 3 days or freeze for up to 1 month. The basil cream will keep in the refrigerator up to 2 days.

SERVE THIS WITH...
Sun-Dried Tomato Bread
  (see page 80)
Cherry & Ricotta Tarts
  (see page 132)
fresh fruit

HEALTH BENEFITS
Red bell peppers contain more vitamin C than oranges—vital for a healthy immune system, lowering cholesterol levels, and regulating blood pressure by thinning the blood. They also contain beta-carotene and flavonoids—antioxidants that strengthen blood capillaries and help fight disease.

# pesto-tuna wraps

The pumpkin seed pesto in these nutritious wraps is rich in heart-protecting omega-3 and omega-6 essential fats. The pesto is extremely versatile—add it to pasta, vegetables, and potato salads, or use it as a dressing.

**SERVES 4**

**PREPARATION**
15 minutes

**STORAGE**
The pesto can be made in advance and kept in the refrigerator up to 1 week. The covered wraps will keep in the refrigerator up to 2 days.

**SERVE THIS WITH...**
Summer Greens with Mango
  Vinaigrette (see page 66)
Amaretto Biscotti (see page 90)
fresh fruit

**HEALTH BENEFITS**
Tuna is an excellent source of protein and although canned tuna lacks the omega-3 fats found in fresh tuna, it still provides useful amounts of vitamins, including B vitamins, that are important for a healthy heart and nervous system, and minerals, such as the antioxidant selenium.

4 reduced-salt tortilla wraps
6oz. canned tuna in water,
  drained and flaked
2 handfuls mixed salad leaves

Pumpkin Seed Pesto:
1 garlic clove, chopped
$1/3$ cup basil
$1/3$ cup pumpkin seeds
5 tbsp. hemp oil or flaxseed oil
2 tbsp. freshly grated
  Parmesan or Gruyère cheese

**1** Put the garlic, basil, and seeds in a food processor and blend 2 to 3 minutes until smooth. With the motor running, add the oil in a thin stream to form a thick sauce, blending for 2 minutes longer. Stir in the cheese.
**2** Spread each tortilla with 1 tbsp. pesto and top with the tuna and salad leaves. Roll tightly into wraps and serve.

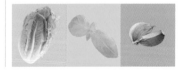

# lime & chili turkey burrito

Lime and chili give this dish a punchy flavor without adding salt. Turkey is a very lean meat that is rich in valuable B vitamins.

1 tbsp. olive oil
3 turkey breast halves, cut into thin strips
1 red chili, seeded and chopped
4 scallions, chopped

juice and grated zest of 1 lime
4 reduced-salt tortilla wraps
1 handful arugula
¼ cup chopped cilantro leaves
¼ cup Greek yogurt

**1** Preheat the oven to 400°F. Heat the oil in a skillet. Add the turkey and chili and stir-fry 5 minutes, or until the turkey is cooked through. Add the scallions and lime and cook 1 minute longer.

**2** Cut out four pieces of foil, each one large enough to completely wrap a tortilla. Put one tortilla on each piece of foil and top with the cooked turkey. Fold the foil over the tortillas to cover and put the foil packages on a baking sheet. Bake 5 to 6 minutes until heated through.

**3** Remove the foil and sprinkle the tortillas with the arugula, cilantro, and yogurt. Roll up tightly and serve.

**SERVES 4**

**PREPARATION + COOKING**
10 + 12 minutes

**STORAGE**
The turkey can be made the day before and kept in the refrigerator overnight. Spoon it over the tortillas and warm through 10 minutes before serving.

**SERVE THIS WITH...**
Asian Coleslaw (see page 67)
Mango & Coconut Tray Bake (see page 88)
fresh fruit

**HEALTH BENEFITS**
Packed with vitamin C, limes are a real boost to the immune system. They also contain potassium, to counter excess sodium intake and balance fluid levels, and limonene, which supports the liver and digestion.

**HEALTH BENEFITS**
Chicken is an excellent low-fat source of protein and it is full of B vitamins—vital for a healthy nervous system, energy production, and preventing cardiovascular disease. It is also rich in the antioxidant selenium and the mineral potassium, which is useful for lowering high blood pressure.

# chicken rice paper wraps

Rice paper wrappers are ideal for anyone with a wheat or gluten sensitivity—and they are a great low-salt option. This tangy garlic and chili sauce is salt-free and incredibly versatile. Protein-rich foods, such as chicken, are most satisfying and filling, so they help prevent midafternoon energy slumps.

20 rice paper wrappers
14oz. roast chicken, cut into
    long strips
4 scallions, finely sliced
1 carrot, peeled and cut into
    matchsticks
½ red bell pepper, seeded and
    cut into thin strips
1 handful bean sprouts

Garlic & Chilli Sauce:
2 tbsp. rice wine vinegar
3 tbsp. honey
1 shallot, chopped
1 red chili, finely chopped
4 garlic cloves, crushed
3 tomatoes, chopped

MAKES 10

PREPARATION + COOKING
30 + 15 minutes

STORAGE
Make the wraps in advance and keep in the refrigerator, covered, up to 2 days. The garlic and chili sauce can be kept in the refrigerator up to 1 week.

**1** To make the sauce, put all the ingredients in a saucepan and bring to a boil. Reduce the heat and simmer 10 to 12 minutes until the mixture begins to thicken. Using an electric hand-held blender, blend until smooth.
**2** Soak 2 rice paper wrappers in warm water 1 to 2 minutes until pliable and opaque. Place them on top of each other on a chopping board. Spread 1 tsp. of the sauce over the top wrapper, then top with a few strips of chicken and vegetables. Roll up both wrappers together, folding in the edges as you roll. Repeat with the remaining wrappers and filling to make 10 wraps.
**3** Serve the wraps with the remaining sauce for dipping.

SERVE THIS WITH...
Asian Coleslaw (see page 67)
Tropical Fruit Skewers
    (see page 139)

Make a large batch of the garlic and chili sauce and use it to coat meats or as an accompaniment to cheese.

026

Ⓥ Ⓞ ⬤ ⬤ ⬤ ⬤

# avocado & tomato bruschetta

A popular Italian appetizer or snack, bruschetta makes a healthy lunch choice, especially when topped with super-nutritious avocado.

**SERVES 4**

**PREPARATION + COOKING**
10 + 5 minutes

**STORAGE**
This is best assembled just before eating.

**SERVE THIS WITH...**
Summer Greens with Mango
  Vinaigrette (see page 66)
Asparagus & Herb Frittata
  (see page 54)
Lemon-Berry Cheesecake
  (see page 130)

**HEALTH BENEFITS**
Avocados are loaded with heart-healthy monounsaturated fat, fiber, vitamin E, folic acid, and iron. They also contain beta-sitosterol, a substance that protects against cancer and can reduce cholesterol. Avocados are one of the richest sources of potassium, essential for balancing body fluids.

2 garlic cloves
1 avocado, peeled, pitted,
   and chopped
1 tomato, chopped
1 tbsp. chopped basil

3 tbsp. olive oil
1 tbsp. balsamic vinegar
4 slices Sun-Dried Tomato
   Bread (see page 80)

**1** Crush one of the garlic cloves and put it in a bowl with the avocado, tomato, basil, 2 tbsp. of the oil, and the vinegar. Stir carefully to combine.
**2** Heat a griddle pan until hot, then add the slices of bread and toast them on both sides. Rub the toasted bread with the remaining garlic clove and drizzle with the remaining oil. Spoon the avocado mixture onto the bread and serve.

# artichoke & onion tarts

MAKES 8/SERVES 8

These little tarts use reduced-salt whole-wheat bread, rather than pastry or regular bread. Artichokes and onions are good sources of potassium to help balance fluid levels and regulate blood pressure.

PREPARATION + COOKING
10 + 25 minutes

STORAGE
Make in advance and keep in the refrigerator up to 3 days.

8 thin slices low-salt whole-wheat bread
2 tbsp. olive oil
½ red onion, chopped
1 garlic clove, crushed

8oz. canned artichoke hearts in water, drained and chopped
3 tbsp. grated Gruyère cheese
3 tbsp. crème fraîche
1 tbsp. chopped basil

SERVE THIS WITH...
Balsamic-Roasted Beets
  (see page 68)
Summer Greens with Mango
  Vinaigrette (see page 66)
Date & Lemon Oat Bars
  (see page 89)
fresh fruit

**1** Preheat the oven to 400°F. Using a 3in. cookie cutter, stamp out 8 circles from the bread. Drizzle 1 tbsp. of the oil over the bread circles, then press each one into a hole in a muffin pan.
**2** Heat the remaining oil in a small skillet. Add the onion and garlic and cook over medium heat 2 to 3 minutes until soft. Tip the onions into a bowl and stir in the artichokes, cheese, crème fraîche, and basil. Spoon the mixture into the bread-lined muffin cups.
**3** Bake 15 to 20 minutes until golden. Serve warm.

HEALTH BENEFITS
Cheese is an excellent source of calcium for strong bones and teeth, but be careful which cheese you choose because many of them are high in salt. Gruyère, Swiss cheese, mozzarella, and ricotta are some of the best low-salt options, or look for reduced-salt versions of your favorites.

028

V O

# asparagus & herb frittata

This nutritious Italian-style omelet is delicious hot or cold and is great for taking on picnics.

2 tbsp. olive oil
4 new potatoes, scrubbed and
   cut into ¼in. slices
1 onion, chopped

12oz. asparagus,
   chargrilled and sliced
3 tbsp. chopped chives
6 eggs, beaten

**1** Heat 1 tbsp. of the oil in an ovenproof skillet with a flameproof handle. Add the potatoes and cook over high heat, stirring, about 5 minutes, or until just soft. Add the onion and cook 2 to 3 minutes longer until soft. Transfer to a bowl and stir in the asparagus, chives, and eggs.
**2** Preheat the broiler to high. Heat the remaining oil in the pan, pour in the egg mixture, and cook over low heat until the top is almost set, about 10 minutes.
**3** Put the pan under the broiler and broil 2 minutes, or until the top is golden. Cut into wedges and serve.

**SERVES 6**

**PREPARATION + COOKING**
10 + 20 minutes

**STORAGE**
Leftovers can be kept in the refrigerator up to 3 days.

**SERVE THIS WITH...**
Balsamic-Roasted Beets
  (see page 68)
Summer Greens with Mango
  Vinaigrette (see page 66)
Summer Berry Crisp
  (see page 134)

**HEALTH BENEFITS**
Asparagus contains the alkaloid asparagine, which stimulates the kidneys and has a strong diuretic affect. Its cleansing properties help combat fluid retention. It is also a good source of folic acid, beta-carotene, vitamin C, and the antioxidant glutathione, which can all help reduce the risk of heart disease.

# corn & pepper fritters

These tasty fritters are sure to be a hit with the whole family—and are a great way of boosting your intake of antioxidant-rich vegetables.

1½ cups self-rising flour
1 tsp. baking powder
2 eggs
½ cup milk or soymilk
8¾oz. canned corn kernels, no added salt or sugar, drained

1 Roasted Pepper (see page 19), chopped
2 scallions, chopped
1 tbsp. chopped parsley
1 tbsp. olive oil

**1** Put the flour, baking powder, eggs, and milk in a bowl. Using an electric mixer, beat until a smooth batter forms. Stir in the corn kernels, pepper, scallions, and parsley.
**2** Heat the oil in a skillet over medium heat until hot. Place 5 tbsp. of the batter in the pan, spacing well apart. Reduce the heat and cook 1 to 2 minutes on each side until golden. Remove the fritters from the pan and keep them warm while you cook the rest of the batter in the same way. Serve warm.

**MAKES 10 TO 12/ SERVES 4**

**PREPARATION + COOKING**
10 + 15 minutes

**STORAGE**
Make in advance and keep in the refrigerator up to 3 days. To reheat, cover with foil and bake at 375°F 5 minutes.

**SERVE THIS WITH...**
Citrus, Bean Sprout & Avocado Salad (see page 63)
lean turkey
Fruit & Seed Loaf (see page 84)
fresh fruit

**HEALTH BENEFITS**
Corn contains plenty of immune-boosting vitamin C and fiber for lowering blood cholesterol. It also provides folic acid and B vitamins, important for boosting energy and combating stress.

⊕

# pan-fried salmon with tomato & bean salad

Salmon is an excellent source of omega-3 fatty acids, which can help prevent heart disease.

**SERVES 4**

**PREPARATION + COOKING**
10 + 10 minutes + marinating

**STORAGE**
Make the dressing in advance and keep in the refrigerator up to 1 week. Get ahead by marinating the salmon in the morning and storing it in the refrigerator until ready to cook.

**SERVE THIS WITH...**
Sun-Dried Tomato Bread
  (see page 80)
Amaretto Biscotti (see page 90)
fresh fruit and yogurt

**HEALTH BENEFITS**
Eating more beans and legumes is a great way to boost your health. High in soluble fiber, they fill you up, stabilize blood sugar levels, and help lower cholesterol. They are also rich in potassium to help balance body fluids and in homocysteine-lowering B vitamins and folic acid.

juice and grated zest
  of ½ lemon
2 tbsp. rice vinegar
2 tbsp. mirin
2 tbsp. olive oil
4 salmon fillets, about
  5oz. each

2 garlic cloves, crushed
9oz. cherry tomatoes, halved
15oz. canned mixed beans,
  no added salt or sugar,
  drained and rinsed
2 tbsp. chopped mint

**1** Whisk together the lemon juice and zest, vinegar, mirin, and 1 tbsp. of the oil. Spoon half this dressing over the salmon and let stand 15 minutes.

**2** Heat the remaining oil in a skillet. Add the fish and cook over high heat 2 to 3 minutes on each side until cooked through. Remove it from the pan and set aside.

**3** Add the garlic to the pan and cook over low heat 2 minutes. Add the tomatoes and beans and cook 2 to 3 minutes longer until the tomatoes start to soften. Add the remaining dressing and cook 1 minute until heated through. Sprinkle with the mint and serve with the fish.

# coconut, shrimp & papaya salad

The coconut in this healthy Thai-inspired salad contains medium-chain triglycerides and manganese to help burn calories and boost energy.

2oz. creamed coconut, grated
½ cup plain yogurt
juice of ½ lemon
a pinch cayenne pepper
2 scallions, chopped
7oz. cooked jumbo shrimp
1 avocado, peeled, pitted,
  and sliced

4 handfuls mixed salad leaves
1 papaya, peeled, seeded,
  and sliced
toasted unsweetened coconut
  flakes, to serve
cilantro leaves, to serve

**1** Put the coconut in a heatproof bowl. Pour 2 tbsp. boiling water over and let cool. Stir in the yogurt, lemon juice, cayenne, and scallions.

**2** Put the shrimp and avocado in a bowl, pour the coconut dressing over, and toss gently.

**3** Divide the salad leaves onto four serving plates, spoon the shrimp mixture over, and top with the sliced papaya. Sprinkle with the coconut flakes and cilantro and serve.

**SERVES 4**

**PREPARATION**
15 minutes

**STORAGE**
This salad is best eaten the day it is made.

**SERVE THIS WITH...**
Spiced Flatbreads (see page 82)
Spice-Poached Pears
  (see page 135)

**HEALTH BENEFITS**
Papaya is a wonderful digestive aid thanks to a powerful enzyme called papain, which helps break down proteins. The fruit is soothing for the gut and, being rich in fiber, it helps control cholesterol levels and relieve constipation. It is also full of skin-friendly beta-carotene.

# crab & fennel salad

Crab is so flavorful there is no need to smother it in creamy, salty dressings. Cucumber is a great diuretic, which is useful for keeping blood pressure down.

**SERVES 4**

**PREPARATION**
15 minutes

**STORAGE**
Make the dressing in advance and keep in the refrigerator up to 2 days.

**SERVE THIS WITH...**
Sesame Crackers (see page 76)
Orange & Cranberry Muffins
  (see page 86)
fresh fruit and yogurt

**HEALTH BENEFITS**
Watercress is packed with antioxidants, including lutein and zeaxanthin for eye health, anticancer glucosinolates and the powerful anti-inflammatory quercepan. It also contains plenty of vitamin C, iron, folic acid, and vitamin B6, needed to make healthy red blood cells and support the immune system.

½ cucumber, seeded and sliced
1 fennel bulb, cored and thinly
  sliced
3½oz. watercress
1lb. 2oz. white crabmeat
freshly ground black pepper

Lemon & Ginger Dressing:
juice and grated zest of
  ½ lemon
1 tsp. honey
1 tbsp. extra virgin olive oil
1 tsp. grated gingerroot
1 tbsp. chopped mint

**1** Put all the dressing ingredients in a small bowl and whisk well.
**2** Put the cucumber, fennel, and watercress in a large bowl, pour the dressing over, and toss.
**3** Season the crab with black pepper and add it to the salad, then serve.

# chicken & artichoke salad

This nutty, subtly sweet vinaigrette supplies plenty of heart-protecting omega fats. The chicken and walnuts are good sources of protein, selenium, and vitamin E for healthy skin and heart.

2 handfuls arugula
2 handfuls mâche or baby
  spinach
3 roasted chicken breast
  halves, shredded
14oz. canned artichoke hearts
  in water, drained and halved
1 small red onion, chopped

6 cherry tomatoes, halved
1 cup walnut pieces, toasted

Walnut Vinaigrette:
3 tbsp. sherry vinegar
5 tbsp. walnut oil
1 tbsp. extra virgin olive oil

**1** Put all the dressing ingredients in a small bowl and whisk well.
**2** Arrange the arugula and mâche on a large serving platter. Sprinkle the chicken, artichokes, onion, tomatoes, and walnuts over, then drizzle with the dressing and serve immediately.

SERVES 4

PREPARATION
15 minutes

STORAGE
Make the dressing the day before and keep it in the refrigerator overnight.

SERVE THIS WITH...
Sun-Dried Tomato Bread
  (see page 80)
Apple Crunch Cake (see page 85)
fresh fruit

HEALTH BENEFITS
Artichokes contain cynarin, a compound that supports the liver, boosting detoxification and digestion. They are also a useful diuretic and can help relieve water retention and regulate blood pressure.

**HEALTH BENEFITS**
Lean beef is an excellent source of iron, which is needed for the manufacture of red blood cells, and zinc, for a healthy immune system. Beef also provides plenty of protein, which is great for giving you an energy boost when you're beginning to flag.

# seared beef & spinach salad

This low-salt, Thai-style salad features a rainbow selection of crunchy vegetables and spinach. It provides a wealth of powerful antioxidants and nutrients to help fight disease.

1lb. 2oz. sirloin steak
1 tbsp. olive oil
2 tbsp. crushed black
   peppercorns
1 carrot, cut into matchsticks
1 red bell pepper, cut into
   matchsticks

1 red onion, thinly sliced
½ cucumber, seeded and
   cut into matchsticks
1 recipe quantity Asian-Style
   Vinaigrette (see page 18)
1 large handful baby spinach
¼ cup chopped cilantro leaves

**SERVES 4**

**PREPARATION + COOKING**
10 + 10 minutes + marinating

**STORAGE**
The dressing can be made
in advance and kept in the
refrigerator up to 1 week.

**SERVE THIS WITH...**
egg or soba noodles
Tropical Fruit Skewers
  (see page 139)

**1** Rub the steaks all over with the oil and peppercorns.
Let marinate 1 hour.

**2** Heat a skillet over high heat until hot. Cook each side
of the steak for 1 minute until brown, then reduce the
heat and cook 3 to 4 minutes on each side until the meat
is cooked but still tender. Remove the steak from the pan
and let rest 10 minutes, then slice it very thinly.

**3** Put the sliced steak in a bowl and add the carrot,
pepper, onion, and cucumber. Pour the vinaigrette over
and toss well.

**4** Put the spinach on a large platter. Top with the beef
salad, sprinkle with the cilantro, and serve immediately.

For a lunchbox,
pack the dressing
separately and add
it right before eating
so the spinach and
other vegetables
stay crisp.

Ⓥ ⊘

# fruity quinoa salad

This salad features a stellar array of flavors and textures, which means there's no need to add salt. Dubbed the "supergrain," quinoa is an excellent protein-rich, gluten-free food.

**SERVES 4 TO 6**

**PREPARATION + COOKING**
10 + 25 minutes

**STORAGE**
Leftover salad can be stored in the refrigerator up to 3 days.

**SERVE THIS WITH...**
Summer Greens with Mango Vinaigrette (see page 66)
Date & Lemon Oat Bars (see page 89)
fresh fruit and yogurt

**HEALTH BENEFITS**
Quinoa is an incredibly nutritious grain, providing plenty of calcium, phosphorus, iron, B vitamins, and vitamin E. Its high fiber content can aid digestion, relieve constipation, and lower cholesterol levels.

heaped ¾ cup quinoa
2 cups Homemade Vegetable Stock (see page 18)
2 tbsp. olive oil
1 red onion, finely chopped
1 tbsp. ground cumin
1 tbsp. ground coriander
1 apple, peeled and finely chopped
½ red bell pepper, seeded and finely chopped
⅓ cup unsalted, roasted cashew nuts
½ cup raisins
⅓ cup dried apricots, chopped
2 tbsp. chopped cilantro leaves

**1** Put the quinoa and vegetable stock in a pan. Bring to a boil, then reduce the heat, cover, and simmer 15 to 20 minutes until the water is absorbed. Remove from the heat and let cool.
**2** Heat the oil in a pan. Add the onion and spices and cook over medium heat 2 to 3 minutes until the onion is soft. Add the onion mixture to the quinoa, then add the apple, pepper, nuts, raisins, apricots, and cilantro. Toss well and serve at room temperature.

# citrus, bean sprout & avocado salad

Citrus fruits, avocado, and crunchy bean sprouts are teamed here in a delicious salad packed with vitamin C and essential fatty acids to help boost the immune system.

2 avocados, peeled, pitted, and sliced
1 grapefruit, peeled and sliced
1 orange, peeled and sliced
1 red onion, finely chopped
1 large handful mixed bean sprouts, such as mung beans and alfalfa sprouts

Dressing:
3 tbsp. orange juice
2 tbsp. hemp or flaxseed oil
1 garlic clove, crushed
1 tsp. honey
2 tbsp. white wine vinegar

**1** Put all the dressing ingredients in a screw-top jar, seal, and shake well.
**2** Put the avocados, grapefruit, orange, onion, and bean sprouts in a large bowl. Pour the dressing over the top and toss gently to coat. Serve immediately.

**SERVES 4**

**PREPARATION**
10 minutes

**STORAGE**
Make the dressing in advance and keep in the refrigerator up to 4 days. The salad is best eaten as soon as possible.

**SERVE THIS WITH...**
Pesto-Tuna Wraps (see page 48)
Cranberry & Date Balls
 (see page 91)
fresh fruit

**HEALTH BENEFITS**
Sprouted beans and seeds are nutritional stars. Concentrated sources of phytonutrients, protein, vitamins, and minerals, they are fantastic energy and immune boosters. Rich in enzymes, they are easily digestible, enabling our bodies to break down and absorb the nutrients. Eat them raw in salads or sandwiches to maximize their nutritional benefits.

037

# spicy stir-fried shrimp

This simple, speedy lunch can be assembled
in the morning and left to marinate in the
refrigerator to let the shrimp absorb the flavor
of the spices. A great protein dish, it will keep
you focused and energized all afternoon.

1lb. large raw shimp, shelled
 and deveined
¼ cup Greek yogurt
2 tbsp. lemon juice
1 garlic clove, crushed
1 tsp. paprika

1 tsp. garam masala
½ tsp. ground cumin
½ tsp. ground coriander
1 tbsp. olive oil
1 tbsp. chopped cilantro leaves

**1** Put the shrimp, yogurt, lemon juice, garlic, and spices
in a bowl and stir well. Cover and chill at least 30 minutes
to let the flavors develop.
**2** Heat the oil in a skillet. Drain the shrimp and add
them to the pan. Stir-fry the shrimp over high heat 3 to
4 minutes until pink and cooked through. Sprinkle with
the cilantro and serve.

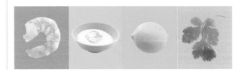

# lemon, chicken & asparagus linguine

Citrus fruit like lemons and limes are a great way of flavoring food instead of using salt.

1 tbsp. olive oil
1 garlic clove, crushed
2 shallots, finely chopped
14oz. boneless chicken breast, cut into bite-size pieces
9oz. asparagus tips, halved lengthwise

juice and grated zest of 1 lemon
14oz. linguine
¼ cup crème fraîche
⅓ cup chopped basil

**SERVES 4**

**PREPARATION + COOKING**
10 + 20 minutes

**STORAGE**
Any leftovers will keep in the refrigerator up to 2 days.

**SERVE THIS WITH...**
mixed salad
Lemon-Berry Cheesecake
  (see page 130)

**HEALTH BENEFITS**
Lemons are an excellent source of immune-boosting vitamin C and antioxidants that help protect the body from damaging free radicals associated with aging. They are also a wonderful cleansing food—begin the day with a glass of hot water and lemon juice to kick-start your digestion.

**1** Heat the oil in a skillet over low heat. Add the garlic and shallots and cook 2 minutes until they begin to soften. Add the chicken and cook 7 to 8 minutes, stirring occasionally, until golden.

**2** Meanwhile, bring a pot of water to a boil. Add the linguine and cook according to the package directions about 8 minutes, or until al dente. Drain well.

**3** Add the asparagus and lemon juice and zest to the chicken and cook 3 to 4 minutes longer until the asparagus is tender. Add the linguine, crème fraîche, and basil. Toss well, heat through, and serve immediately.

# summer greens with mango vinaigrette

**SERVES 4**

**PREPARATION**
15 minutes

**STORAGE:**
Make the dressing in advance
and keep it in the refrigerator
up to 3 days.

**SERVE THIS WITH...**
Artichoke & Onion Tarts
  (see page 53)
Summer Berry Crisp
  (see page 134)

**HEALTH BENEFITS**
The mango's gorgeous orange-
yellow color highlights their
beta-carotene content, important
for healthy skin and immune
system. They also provide
plenty of vitamin C, vitamin
E, and potassium—good for
strengthening blood vessels
and protecting the heart.

This delicious, refreshing salad is tossed in
a fruity dressing bursting with antioxidants and
essential fatty acids. Include a variety of salad
greens for maximum nutrition.

10oz. mixed salad greens
1 mango, peeled, pitted,
  and sliced
1 small red onion, finely
  chopped
½ cucumber, seeded and sliced

Mango Vinaigrette:
1 mango, peeled, pitted,
  and sliced
juice and grated zest of 1 lemon
1 garlic clove, crushed
1 tsp. honey
2 tbsp. raspberry vinegar
3 tbsp. flaxseed or hemp oil

**1** Put all the vinaigrette ingredients in a blender and blend
2 to 3 minutes until smooth.
**2** Put the salad greens, mango, onion, and cucumber in
a bowl. Pour the dressing over the top and toss gently
to mix. Serve immediately.

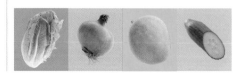

# asian coleslaw

Most mayonnaise-based sauces are high in saturated fat and salt. The Asian-inspired dressing used here features a number of flavorful exotic spices that are enriched with a little heart-healthy olive oil. This coleslaw makes a delicious accompaniment to broiled or grilled meats and fish or spicy burgers.

1 tbsp. extra virgin olive oil
1 recipe quantity Asian-Style Vinaigrette (see page 18)
3 cups finely shredded red cabbage
2 carrots, peeled and grated
1 red bell pepper, seeded and thinly sliced
1 cup bean sprouts
4 scallions, thinly sliced

**1** Stir the olive oil into the vinaigrette.
**2** Put the cabbage, carrot, pepper, bean sprouts, and scallions in a serving bowl and toss to mix. Pour the vinaigrette over the top and let stand 15 minutes, then stir and serve.

**SERVES 4**

**PREPARATION**
15 minutes

**STORAGE**
Make in advance and keep in the refrigerator up to 4 days.

**SERVE THIS WITH...**
Thai Crab Cakes (see page 97)
Mango & Coconut Tray Bake (see page 88)
fresh fruit

**HEALTH BENEFITS**
Cabbage contains a range of powerful sulfurous substances, including glucosinolates that help protect against certain cancers and enhance the liver's detoxing capacity. It is also rich in vitamin C, fiber, folic acid, and potassium—all valuable nutrients for maintaining a healthy heart.

# balsamic-roasted beets

**SERVES 4**

**PREPARATION + COOKING**
10 + 40 minutes

**STORAGE**
The beets can be cooked in advance and served hot or cold. Keep leftovers in the refrigerator up to 3 days.

**SERVE THIS WITH...**
Baked Sesame Trout
(see page 102)
Orange-Honey Sweet Potatoes
(see page 71)
Lemon-Berry Cheesecake
(see page 130)

**HEALTH BENEFITS**
Beets are a great cleansing food and can boost the liver's detoxifying properties. Rich in soluble fiber, it can also help lower cholesterol. Being naturally high in sugars and iron, beets keep you feeling energized and boost concentration.

Forget pickled beets—fresh roasted beets have an incomparable sweet, earthy flavor that doesn't need to be loaded down with salt. Great blood purifiers, beets also contains a wealth of powerful antioxidants.

8 baby beets or 4 medium
   beets, peeled
3 tbsp. balsamic vinegar
¼ cup olive oil

juice of ½ orange
1 garlic clove, crushed
1 tsp. chopped rosemary
freshly ground black pepper

**1** Preheat the oven to 400°F. Cut the medium beets, if using, in half. Place a sheet of foil on a baking sheet and arrange the beets on top.
**2** Put the remaining ingredients in a bowl and whisk well. Drizzle the mixture over the beets, then gather up the foil to form a package and seal. Roast 40 minutes, or until the beets are tender, then serve.

# mint & lemon zucchini

The lemon dressing in this summery dish is a great alternative to salt and can be paired with other broiled or steamed vegetables. Using flaxseed or hemp oil is a good way to get healthy omega fats into your diet.

4 zucchini, thinly sliced
   lengthwise
1 tbsp. olive oil
freshly ground black pepper

**Lemon & Mint Dressing:**
2 tbsp. lemon juice
1 tsp. grated lemon zest
2 tsp. honey
¼ cup hemp or flaxseed oil
1 handful mint, chopped

**SERVES 4**

**PREPARATION + COOKING**
10 + 20 minutes

**STORAGE**
Leftovers will keep in the refrigerator up to 2 days.

**SERVE THIS WITH...**
Lamb Koftas with Mint Yogurt
  (see page 114)
whole-wheat pita bread
Cherry & Ricotta Tarts
  (see page 132)

**HEALTH BENEFITS**
Peppermint contains menthol, a volatile oil that is useful for clearing congestion. It also promotes the secretion of digestive juices and has calming and anti-inflammatory properties to soothe an irritable bowel.

**1** Put all the ingredients for the dressing in a bowl and whisk well.

**2** Put the zucchini in another bowl and drizzle with the olive oil, then season with black pepper.

**3** Heat a griddle pan or skillet until hot. Add the zucchini and cook, in batches, 2 to 3 minutes on each side until golden brown.

**4** Put the griddled zucchini in a clean bowl, pour the dressing over while they are still warm, and toss gently. Serve warm or at room temperature.

# chili & sesame broccoli

Quickly stir-frying vegetables is a great way of retaining their nutrients and maximizing their natural flavors without adding salt. Sesame seeds increase the protein content of this dish and provide health-promoting omega-6 and omega-9 fatty acids.

**SERVES 4**

**PREPARATION + COOKING**
10 + 10 minutes

**STORAGE**
Best eaten immediately.

**SERVE THIS WITH...**
Vietnamese Pork Noodles
(see page 112)
Tropical Fruit Skewers
(see page 139)

**HEALTH BENEFITS**
Broccoli is a superfood for the heart and immune system. It is an excellent source of antioxidants and fiber to help lower cholesterol. It is also high in folic acid, which is useful for reducing levels of homocysteine in the blood. Like other cruciferous vegetables, it contains glucosinolates, which have powerful detoxifying and anticancer properties.

3 tsp. sesame seeds
2 tbsp. olive oil
1 shallot, finely chopped
1 red chili, seeded and finely chopped
2 garlic cloves, crushed
1lb. broccoli, cut into small florets
toasted sesame oil, to serve

**1** Heat a nonstick pan over medium heat until hot. Add the sesame seeds and toast 1 to 2 minutes until golden. Watch them carefully so they do not burn. Remove from the heat and set aside.

**2** Heat the olive oil in a large skillet or wok over low heat. Add the shallot, chili, and garlic and cook 2 to 3 minutes until soft.

**3** Add the broccoli and 1 tbsp. water and stir-fry 3 to 4 minutes until just soft. Scatter the toasted sesame seeds over, drizzle with sesame oil, and serve.

# orange-honey sweet potatoes

Incredibly nutrient-rich, sweet potatoes are digested more slowly than other potatoes, helping to maintain energy levels for longer.

2 tbsp. olive oil
2 tbsp. honey
3 tbsp. orange juice

4 sweet potatoes, peeled and
cut into wedges
freshly ground black pepper

**1** Preheat the oven to 400°F. Put the oil, honey, and orange juice in a small bowl and season to taste with black pepper. Whisk well.
**2** Put the sweet potatoes in a roasting pan, pour the honey mixture over the top, and toss well to coat.
**3** Roast 30 to 40 minutes until brown and tender, occasionally spooning the released juices over the sweet potatoes to baste. Serve hot.

**SERVES 4**

**PREPARATION + COOKING**
10 + 40 minutes

**STORAGE**
Leftovers will keep in the refrigerator up to 2 days.

**SERVE THIS WITH...**
Apricot-Turkey Burgers
(see page 107)
mixed salad
Summer Berry Crisp
(see page 134)

**HEALTH BENEFITS**
Orange-fleshed sweet potatoes are teeming with antioxidants, particularly beta-carotene and vitamin C, which help protect the body against the effects of aging. They are also a good source of vitamin E, vital for a healthy heart and skin. Their high fiber content can help lower cholesterol and aid digestive health.

**045**

# roasted lemon-paprika new potatoes

This delicious recipe enhances the flavor of roasted potatoes without the need for salt or creamy dressings.

**SERVES 4 TO 6**

**PREPARATION + COOKING**
10 + 30 minutes

**STORAGE**
Leftovers can be kept in the refrigerator up to 3 days.

**SERVE THIS WITH...**
Roasted Vegetables & Dukkah
  (see page 123)
fresh fruit and yogurt
Cranberry & Date Balls
  (see page 91)

**HEALTH BENEFITS**
New potatoes are a rich source of vitamin C and B vitamins, which are needed for energy production. Most of their fiber, vitamins, and minerals are found in the skin, so choose organic potatoes, if possible, and leave the skin on.

| | |
|---|---|
| 2lb. 4oz. baby new potatoes, scrubbed | 1 tsp. cumin seeds, lightly ground |
| 3 tbsp. olive oil | 1 tsp. smoked paprika |
| juice and grated zest of 1 lemon | freshly ground black pepper |

**1** Preheat the oven to 400°F. Cook the potatoes in boiling water 5 minutes, or just until they start to turn tender. Drain well, then transfer to a baking sheet.

**2** Put the oil, lemon juice and zest, cumin, and paprika in a small bowl. Season to taste with black pepper and whisk. Pour over the potatoes and toss to coat.

**3** Bake 20 to 25 minutes until golden and tender, occasionally spooning the released juices over the potatoes to baste. Serve hot or cold.

# coconut rice

This creamy, lightly spiced rice is the perfect accompaniment to curries and Asian dishes. Warming and wonderfully satisfying, it is sure to become a favorite with the whole family.

2 tbsp. olive oil
1 onion, finely chopped
2 garlic cloves, crushed
4 cardamom pods, crushed

1¼ cups brown basmati rice, rinsed
1¼ cups coconut milk
1 small handful cilantro leaves, chopped

**1** Heat the oil in a large pan. Add the onion and garlic and fry over medium heat 2 to 3 minutes until soft. Add the cardamom pods and rice and stir to coat in the oil.
**2** Pour in the coconut milk and scant ½ cup water. Bring to a boil, then reduce the heat and simmer 20 minutes until all the liquid is absorbed.
**3** Sprinkle with the cilantro and serve.

**SERVES 4**

**PREPARATION + COOKING**
5 + 25 minutes

**STORAGE**
Leftovers will keep in the refrigerator up to 2 days.

**SERVE THIS WITH...**
Chicken Tikka (see page 106)
Chili & Sesame Broccoli
  (see page 70)
Spice-Poached Pears
  (see page 135)

**HEALTH BENEFITS**
Brown basmati rice is an excellent source of cholesterol-lowering fiber, B vitamins, and manganese, which can help stabilize blood sugar levels. It releases its sugars more slowly than white rice, so it will keep you feeling fuller longer.

# SNACKS

One of the best ways to cut down on salt is to avoid processed foods, since the majority of salt we consume is "hidden" in commercial products. Breads, cakes, cookies, pastries, and other sweet treats can be very high in salt. But make your own with these delicious, easy-to-follow recipes and you won't need to go without. Choose from a delectable selection of savory options that include Sun-Dried Tomato Bread, Spicy Tortilla Chips, or Pumpkin & Seed Loaf; or satisfy a sweet tooth with a range of great-tasting treats, such as Orange & Cranberry Muffins, Amaretto Biscotti, or Mango & Coconut Bars. These recipes are full of nutritious ingredients and bursting with natural flavors—so you certainly won't feel deprived.

# sesame crackers

These homemade crackers get their flavor from smoked paprika and sesame seeds, rather than from added salt.

1 cup whole-wheat flour
1 cup all-purpose flour, plus
    extra for rolling
1 tsp. baking powder
½ tsp. smoked paprika
3 tbsp. grated low-salt cheese,
    such as Swiss cheese

¼ cup sesame seeds
¼ cup olive oil
scant 1 cup milk, plus extra
    for brushing

**1** Preheat the oven to 375°F. Put both flours, the baking powder, paprika, cheese, and half the sesame seeds in a bowl. Add the oil and ¼ cup of the milk and mix together with your hands. Gradually add more milk and continue mixing until a soft dough forms.

**2** Put the dough on a lightly floured surface. Roll it out to ¾in. thick, then cut out 15 to 20 circles with a 3in. cookie cutter. Put the circles on a baking sheet, brush the tops with a little milk, and sprinkle the remaining sesame seeds over.

**3** Bake 10 to 12 minutes until golden brown. Let cool on the baking sheet 1 minute, then transfer to a wire rack to cool completely.

**MAKES 15 TO 20**

**PREPARATION + COOKING**
15 + 12 minutes

**STORAGE**
Keep in an airtight container up to 4 days or freeze up to 1 month.

**SERVE THIS WITH...**
Roasted Red Pepper Hummus (see page 42)
Sun-Dried Tomato Dip (see page 43)
Orange & Cranberry Muffins (see page 86)
fresh fruit

**HEALTH BENEFITS**
Whole-wheat flour is much higher in fiber and B vitamins than white refined versions. It also releases energy more slowly, keeping you feeling fuller for longer and helping to avoid energy slumps during the day.

# roasted spiced nuts

You can avoid the temptation to reach for a bag of salted nuts with this delicious, spicy, salt-free recipe. These nuts are simple to prepare—and incredibly addictive. They are great as a snack on their own or sprinkled over salads to add extra crunch.

2 tbsp. olive oil
1½ cups unsalted mixed nuts, such as Brazil nuts, pecans, almonds, cashews, and peanuts

¼ tsp. garam masala
¼ tsp. cayenne

**1** Heat the oil in a skillet. Add the nuts and fry 2 to 3 minutes, stirring occasionally, until they start to turn golden. You might have to do this in batches.
**2** Transfer the nuts to a bowl, sprinkle the spices over the top, and toss well to coat. Let cool before serving.

**SERVES 4**

**PREPARATION + COOKING**
5 + 6 minutes

**STORAGE**
Make in advance and keep in an airtight container in the refrigerator up to 1 week.

**SERVE THIS WITH...**
Moroccan Burgers
  (see page 115)
whole-wheat rolls
mixed salad

**HEALTH BENEFITS**
Nuts are a great energizing, protein-rich food. Brazil nuts are exceptionally high in selenium, important for the immune system and healthy thyroid and sperm. They also contain plenty of heart-friendly omega-3 and omega-6 fatty acids, plus healthy monounsaturated fats.

049

V O Ø Ø

# spicy tortilla chips

A healthy alternative to traditional salty chips, these are simple to prepare and delicious dipped into homemade salsas or dips. To make these gluten-free, use 100 percent corn tortillas.

**SERVES 4**

**PREPARATION + COOKING**
5 + 10 minutes

**STORAGE**
Make in advance and keep in an airtight container for up to 4 days.

**SERVE THIS WITH...**
Baked Eggs with Harissa
  (see page 38)
Roasted Red Pepper Hummus
  (see page 42)
Sun-Dried Tomato Dip
  (see page 43)

**HEALTH BENEFITS**
Whole-wheat breads, rolls, and tortillas contain unrefined complex carbohydrates, which release their energy more slowly than white, processed versions. Choose reduced-salt varieties to keep salt levels to a minimum.

1 egg white, lightly beaten
2 tbsp. olive oil
1 tsp. Dijon mustard
1 garlic clove, crushed

½ tsp. chili powder
½ tsp. cayenne pepper
3 low-salt soft corn or whole-
  wheat tortillas

**1** Preheat the oven to 350°F. Put the egg white, oil, mustard, garlic, chili powder, and cayenne in a bowl and whisk well. Brush one side of each tortilla with the egg mixture. Cut the tortillas into wedges and put them, brushed-side up, on a baking sheet.
**2** Bake 5 to 10 minutes until crisp. Remove from the oven, transfer to a wire rack, and let cool.

# pumpkin & seed loaf

This quick recipe yields a light bread that is delicious served with soup or stews or lightly toasted for a healthy snack. Canned pumpkin pie filling is a great pantry ingredient that is also rich in immune-boosting antioxidants.

2 cups self-rising flour
2 tsp. baking powder
a pinch cayenne pepper
½ cup mixed seeds, such as sesame, sunflower, and pumpkin
5 tbsp. milk

2 tbsp. honey
1 egg, lightly beaten
2 tbsp. olive oil, plus extra for greasing
scant 1 cup canned pumpkin pie mix

**MAKES 1 LOAF**

**PREPARATION + COOKING**
15 + 30 minutes

**STORAGE**
Make in advance, wrap, and keep in the refrigerator up to 3 days or freeze up to 1 month.

**SERVE THIS WITH…**
Roasted Garlic & Tomato Soup (see page 45)
salads
Chocolate & Orange Soufflés (see page 133)

**HEALTH BENEFITS**
Pumpkins are a good source of carotenoids, which protect against cancer and heart disease. They also provide plenty of fiber, useful for lowering cholesterol and improving digestion.

**1** Preheat the oven to 375°F. Put the flour, baking powder, cayenne, and half the seeds in a bowl and mix well. In a separate bowl, mix together the milk, honey, egg, and oil. Add this to the dry ingredients and stir with a wooden spoon until well mixed.
**2** Tip the batter into a lightly greased 1lb. loaf pan, then sprinkle the remaining seeds over.
**3** Bake 30 minutes, or until golden brown and a skewer inserted into the middle of the loaf comes out clean. Let the loaf cool in the pan 5 minutes, then transfer it to a wire rack to cool completely before slicing and serving.

051

# sun-dried tomato bread

**HEALTH BENEFITS**
Tomatoes and olive oil are a very healthy combination. Carotenoids, abundant in tomatoes, are fat-soluble, which means they need to be eaten with a little fat to be absorbed. Olive oil is also a good source of healthy monounsaturates, useful for protecting against heart disease.

This delicious Italian bread combines sun-dried tomatoes and toasted nuts to produce a wonderful rich flavor without the need for any salt. The tomatoes not only add a beautiful color, they are also packed full of carotenoids, important nutrients for the skin and eyes which also offer protection against certain cancers. For a gluten-free version, use a gluten-free flour mix.

4 cups whole-wheat bread flour
¼oz. fast-acting dry yeast
½ cup toasted nuts
8 sun-dried tomatoes in oil,
    drained and chopped
2 eggs

1 tbsp. low-salt sun-dried
    tomato paste
¼ cup olive oil, plus extra
    for greasing
1 tbsp. honey

**MAKES 1 LARGE LOAF**

**PREPARATION + COOKING**
20 + 30 minutes + rising

**STORAGE**
Make the bread in advance,
wrap in plastic wrap or foil,
and keep in an airtight container
up to 3 days or freeze up to
1 month.

**SERVE THIS WITH...**
Chicken & Artichoke Salad
(see page 59)

**1** Put the flour, yeast, nuts, and tomatoes in a large bowl. Stir, then make a well in the middle of the mixture.
**2** In a separate bowl, mix together the eggs, tomato paste, oil, and honey. Pour the egg mixture into the well in the flour and mix together, using your hands. Gradually add 1¼ cups warm water and continue mixing until a soft dough forms. Knead in the bowl 10 minutes until elastic, then cover and let rise 1 hour.
**3** Punch down the dough, knead again for a few minutes, and shape into a large round loaf. Put the loaf on a lightly oiled baking sheet, cover, and let rise 20 minutes. Preheat the oven to 425°F
**4** Bake 30 minutes, or until golden. Remove from the oven and transfer to a wire rack to cool completely before serving.

Toasting nuts is
a great way to enhance
their natural, sweet
flavor, so there's no
need for salt or other
additives.

# spiced flatbreads

Completely salt-free, yet full of flavor, these Indian flatbreads are perfect for dipping into tagines and curries.

**MAKES 10**

**PREPARATION + COOKING**
25 + 20 minutes + rising

**STORAGE**
Make in advance, wrap, and keep in an airtight container up to 3 days or freeze up to 1 month. Warm through in the oven from frozen.

**SERVE THIS WITH…**
Vegetable Tagine with Dates & Almonds (se page 124)
Rose Water Rice Pudding with Strawberries (see page 128)

**HEALTH BENEFITS**
Many Indian spices are known for their healing properties. Cumin is a useful digestive aid and helps the body absorb nutrients. It can also stimulate the immune system and have an antimucosal effect, helping to clear coughs and colds.

¾oz. fast-acting dry yeast
2 tbsp. honey
1 tbsp. cumin seeds, dry-roasted and ground
1 tbsp. coriander seeds, dry-roasted and ground
1 tbsp. sesame seeds

4 cups white bread flour
3½ cups whole-wheat bread flour
olive oil, for greasing

**1** Put the yeast, honey, and 1¼ cups lukewarm water in a bowl and stir until the yeast dissolves. Set aside 15 minutes.

**2** Put the ground spices, sesame seeds, and flours in a large bowl. Add the yeast mixture and an additional 1¼ cups lukewarm water and mix, using your hands, until the mixture forms a soft dough. Knead briefly, then cover the bowl and let rise 1 hour.

**3** Preheat the oven to 425°F. Divide the dough into 10 equal pieces and roll each one into a thin oval. Put them on lightly greased baking sheets and bake 5 to 10 minutes until puffed up and golden. Transfer to a wire rack and let cool completely before serving.

# chili-corn muffins

Cornmeal is high in B vitamins, which can help the body to cope with stress.

2¼ cups cornmeal
scant 1 cup. all-purpose flour
2 tsp. baking powder
½ tsp. cayenne pepper
½ cup canned corn kernels,
    no added salt or sugar

2 eggs, beaten
½ cup olive oil, plus extra
    for greasing
²/₃ cup milk

**1** Preheat the oven to 375°F. Put the cornmeal, flour, baking powder, cayenne, and corn kernels in a bowl. In another bowl, mix together the eggs, oil, and milk. Pour this into the flour and stir briefly until a batter forms.
**2** Divide the mixture into six to eight holes of a lightly greased muffin pan. Bake 20 to 30 minutes until golden and firm to the touch. Let the muffins cool in the pan 1 minute, then transfer to a wire rack and let cool completely before serving.

**MAKES 6 TO 8 MUFFINS**

**PREPARATION + COOKING**
15 + 30 minutes

**STORAGE**
Make in advance and keep in an airtight container up to 3 days or freeze up to 1 month.

**SERVE THIS WITH...**
Roasted Garlic & Tomato Soup
  (see page 45)
mixed salad
Baked Pear & Spice Puddings
  (see page 129)

**HEALTH BENEFITS**
Cornmeal is a rich source of energy-giving carbohydrates, fiber, potassium, and B vitamins—useful for balancing blood sugar levels and great for appetite control.

# fruit & seed loaf

This delicious, fat-free quick bread is bursting with omega-rich seeds, warming spices, and dried fruit. Soy flour and soymilk provide a heap of health-boosting phytoestrogen.

**MAKES 1 LOAF**

**PREPARATION + COOKING**
15 + 70 minutes + soaking

**STORAGE**
Make in advance, wrap in foil, and keep in the refrigerator up to 4 days or freeze up to 1 month.

**SERVE THIS WITH...**
Cranberry & Cherry Compote
(see page 25)
Asparagus & Herb Frittata
(see page 54)
mixed salad
fresh fruit

**HEALTH BENEFITS**
Pumpkin seeds contain both omega-3 and omega-6 fatty acids and plenty of micro-nutrients like vitamin E and zinc, important for the immune system and healthy, glowing skin. They also contain calcium and magnesium, which are needed for strong bones and to relax muscles and blood vessels.

1 cup plus 2 tbsp. soy flour
1 cup self-rising flour
2 tsp. baking powder
1 piece candied ginger, chopped
1 tsp. ground cinnamon

scant 1²/₃ cups mixed seeds, such as pumpkin, sunflower, and flaxseed
²/₃ cup raisins
²/₃ cup mixed dried berries
2 cups soymilk
¼ cup honey
scant ½ cup apple sauce

**1** Put both flours, baking powder, ginger, cinnamon, seeds, and dried fruit in a large bowl. Put the soymilk, honey, and apple sauce in a saucepan and heat over low heat until warm. Stir into the flour mixture and let stand 30 minutes. Preheat the oven to 325°F.
**2** Spoon the mixture into a lightly greased 2lb. loaf pan. Bake 60 to 70 minutes until golden brown and a skewer inserted into the middle of the loaf comes out clean. Let cool completely in the pan before turning out and serving.

# apple crunch cake

This delicious cake, full of slow-releasing energy from the oats, whole-wheat flour, and apples, keeps hunger pangs at bay.

4½ cups peeled, cored, and
    sliced apples
1¼ cups plus heaped 2 tbsp.
    self-rising flour
1 cup rolled oats

scant 2 cups muesli, no added
    salt or sugar
1 tsp. ground ginger
3 tbsp. honey
¼ cup olive oil
²/₃ cup plain yogurt

**1** Preheat the oven to 375°F. Put the apples in a saucepan with 3 tbsp. water, cover, and simmer over medium heat 5 minutes until soft. Transfer to a blender and blend 1 to 2 minutes until smooth.

**2** Put the flour, rolled oats, muesli, and ginger in a bowl, then mix in the honey, oil, and yogurt.

**3** Press half the oat mixture into a lightly greased 8in. loose-bottom cake pan. Bake 15 minutes until golden. Remove from the oven, spoon the apple puree over the top, and sprinkle with the remaining oat mixture, then bake 30 to 35 minutes longer until golden.

**4** Let cool completely on a wire rack. Slice and serve at room temperature.

**SERVES 8**

**PREPARATION + COOKING**
15 + 55 minutes

**STORAGE**
Make in advance and keep in the refrigerator up to 2 days.

**SERVE THIS WITH...**
Pan-Fried Salmon with Tomato
  & Bean Salad (see page 56)
mixed salad
fresh fruit

**HEALTH BENEFITS**
Quercetin, an antioxidant found in many fruit and vegetables, including apples, helps protect cholesterol from oxidation and accumulating in the arteries. It is also known for its anti-inflammatory properties, making it useful for conditions such as arthritis, asthma, and allergies.

# orange & cranberry muffins

**HEALTH BENEFITS**
All berries are packed full of antioxidants, particularly anthocyanins, as well as vitamin C to keep the immune system healthy. Cranberries and blueberries contain natural antibacterial properties that can help prevent and treat urinary tract infections, such as cystitis.

These muffins make a great high-fiber treat without the added salt found in many varieties you buy. Oat bran and flaxseeds are rich in soluble fiber, which can help regulate blood sugar levels and maintain a healthy bowel. Flaxseeds are an excellent source of essential fatty acids.

¾ cup plus 2 heaped tbsp.
   all-purpose flour
½ cup oat bran
7 tbsp. ground flaxseed
2 tsp. baking powder
1 orange, peeled and sliced
   with seeds removed

½ cup fructose
scant ½ cup buttermilk or
   plain yogurt
¼ cup olive oil, plus extra
   for greasing
1 egg, beaten
¹/₃ cup dried cranberries

**1** Preheat the oven to 350°F. Put the flour, oat bran,
flaxseed, and baking powder in a bowl and mix together.
**2** Put the orange, fructose, buttermilk, oil, and egg
in a blender and blend until smooth. Add this mixture into
the dry ingredients, add the cranberries, and stir briefly.
**3** Divide the mixture into 12 holes of a lightly greased
muffin pan. Bake 20 minutes, or until golden brown
and firm to the touch. Let the muffins cool in the pan
1 minute, then transfer to a wire rack. Serve warm or
at room temperature.

**MAKES 12**

**PREPARATION + COOKING**
15 + 20 minutes

**STORAGE**
Make in advance and keep
in an airtight container in the
refrigerator up to 4 days or
freeze up to 1 month.

**SERVE THIS WITH...**
Apricot Turkey Burgers
  (see page 107)
fresh fruit

> Oranges are a
> great source of
> vitamin C and contain
> beta-sitosterol, a
> plant sterol shown to
> lower cholesterol.

Ⓥ 🖉 🖉 🖉 🖉

# mango & coconut bars

These salt-free bars, packed with the natural flavors of mango and coconut, are a nutritious, tropical snack the kids will love.

**MAKES 16**

**PREPARATION + COOKING**
10 + 35 minutes + soaking

**STORAGE**
Make in advance and keep in an airtight container in the refrigerator up to 4 days or freeze up to 1 month.

**SERVE THIS WITH...**
Seared Beef & Spinach Salad (see page 60)
egg or rice noodles
fresh fruit

**HEALTH BENEFITS**
Dried exotic fruit like mango and papaya make the perfect healthy snack. They are a rich source of potassium, important for balancing body fluids and lowering blood pressure.

4oz. dried mango slices, without sugar, chopped
2 ripe mangos, peeled, seeded, and sliced
juice and grated zest of 3 limes
²/₃ cup olive oil
½ cup rolled oats
2¼ cups plus 2 tbsp. self-rising flour
1 tsp. baking powder
1 cup shredded coconut

**1** Preheat the oven to 350°F. Put the dried mango in a heatproof bowl, cover with boiling water, and let soak 30 minutes, then drain.
**2** Put the fresh mango, lime juice and zest, and oil in a blender and blend for 1 to 2 minutes until smooth.
**3** Put the oats, flours, baking powder, coconut, and dried mango in a bowl and mix well. Stir in the mango puree.
**4** Spoon the batter into a lightly greased 10 x 12in. baking pan and smooth the surface. Bake 30 to 35 minutes until golden brown. Let cool in the pan, then cut into 16 slices and serve.

# date & lemon oat bars

Snack bars can often be high in salt, so this tangy, homemade version is a great alternative.

juice and grated zest of
   4 lemons
6 tbsp. apple juice
2 cups chopped dried pitted
   dates
5 tbsp. honey
²/₃ cup olive oil, plus extra
   for greasing

1½ cups rolled oats
1¼ cups plus heaped 2 tbsp.
   self-rising flour
¼ cup sunflower seeds
½ tsp. baking soda
scant 1 cup finely ground
   blanched almonds

**1** Preheat the oven to 350°F. Put the lemon juice and zest, apple juice, and 1⅓ cups of the dates in a pan. Simmer over medium heat 1 to 2 minutes, stirring, then set aside to cool. Pour the mixture into a blender, add the honey and oil, and blend until smooth.

**2** Put all the remaining ingredients in a bowl and stir in the date puree. Press the mixture into a lightly greased 10 x 12in. baking pan. Bake 25 to 30 minutes until golden, then let cool. Cut into 16 bars and serve.

**MAKES 16**

**PREPARATION + COOKING**
15 + 35 minutes

**STORAGE**
Make in advance and keep in an airtight container in the refrigerator up to 5 days or freeze up to 1 month.

**SERVE THIS WITH…**
Lamb Koftas with Mint Yogurt
  (see page 114)
Citrus, Bean Sprout & Avocado
  Salad (see page 63)
fresh fruit

**HEALTH BENEFITS**
Full of natural sugars and iron, dates make a good choice for flagging energy levels. They also provide plenty of potassium, which can help regulate blood pressure. Using whole-wheat flour and rolled oats slows down the rate at which the sugars are released into the bloodstream, leaving you feeling fuller longer.

# amaretto biscotti

These crisp almond and apricot cookies, laced with amaretto, are a healthy, yet indulgent, treat. Serve them with coffee in place of dessert or with sorbets and ice creams.

**MAKES 16**

**PREPARATION + COOKING**
15 + 45 minutes

**STORAGE**
Make in advance and keep in an airtight container up to 1 week.

**SERVE THIS WITH...**
Seared Salmon with Gremolata (see page 100)
Sun-Dried Tomato Bread (see page 80)
mixed salad
Pomegranate-Orange Sorbet (see page 136)

**HEALTH BENEFITS**
Dried apricots are rich in lycopene and beta-carotene, important for a healthy heart, skin, and eyes. They also provide plenty of iron, which can help prevent anemia. Avoid bright orange dried apricots as they have been treated with sulfur.

¾ cup plus 4½ tsp. all-purpose flour
1 tsp. baking powder
⅓ cup fructose
scant ½ cup chopped dried apricots

⅓ cup chopped blanched almonds
1 egg, beaten
1 tbsp. amaretto liqueur
vegetable oil, for greasing

**1** Preheat the oven to 350°F. Line a baking sheet with baking parchment. Put the flour, baking powder, fructose, apricots, and almonds in a bowl. Add the egg and amaretto and stir until a soft dough forms.

**2** Roll the mixture into a long log about 2in. wide and place on a lightly greased baking sheet. Bake 25 minutes, or until golden.

**3** Remove from the oven but leave the oven on. Let the log cool 10 minutes, then cut the cylinder at an angle into ¼in. slices. Arrange the biscotti on the baking sheet and bake 8 to 10 minutes on each side until crisp. Transfer to a wire rack to cool, then serve.

# cranberry & date balls

Rather than snacking on candy and chocolate, which can contain added salt, choose these delicious, energy-boosting morsels when you want a treat.

¾ cup dried cranberries
⅓ cup dried pitted dates
1 tbsp. apple juice

2 to 3 tbsp. finely ground
  blanched almonds
½ cup shredded coconut

**1** Put the cranberries, dates, and apple juice in a food processor and blend until smooth. Add enough of the ground almonds to form a stiff paste.
**2** Shape teaspoons of the mixture into 10 to 12 balls of equal size and roll them in the coconut to coat. Chill until required, then serve.

**MAKES 10 TO 12**

**PREPARATION**
15 minutes

**STORAGE**
Make in advance and keep in the refrigerator for up to 1 week.

**SERVE THIS WITH...**
Pesto-Tuna Wraps (see page 48)
fresh fruit and yogurt

**HEALTH BENEFITS**
Dried fruit contains plenty of antioxidants, B vitamins, and iron, and, since it is naturally sweet, there is no need to add extra sugar. Rich in potassium, it can help lower blood pressure and reduce fluid retention.

# DINNERS

Takeout and prepared meals can be tempting at the end of a long day, but they often contain more salt than your whole day's recommended amount, not to mention excess calories and fat. Creating a delicious, satisfying evening meal that is also low in salt doesn't need to be a struggle or take hours to prepare. This chapter is packed with mouthwatering main courses, such as Apricot Turkey Burgers and Pesto-Crusted Chicken, which are sure to be a hit with the kids. There are plenty of speedy weekday dishes, such as Baked Sesame Trout; vegetarian delights like Sweet Potato & Coconut Curry; and more indulgent meals, such as Roasted Quail with Pomegranate Molasses. All these fabulous, low-salt dishes will delight your family and friends.

**061**

SERVES 4

PREPARATION + COOKING
10 + 10 minutes

STORAGE
Best eaten on the day they
are made.

SERVE THIS WITH...
Citrus, Bean Sprout & Avocado
Salad (see page 63)
Apple Crunch Cake (see page 85)
fresh fruit

HEALTH BENEFITS
Many herbs have healing
properties and contain a
wealth of minerals. Basil is rich
in flavonoids and volatile oils,
which have antibacterial and
anti-inflammatory properties.
It also contains magnesium
and potassium to help relax
blood vessels and muscles
and regulate blood pressure.

# scallops en papillote

Cooking seafood in parchment or foil bags
helps retain all the flavor and nutrients.

1 tbsp. olive oil, plus extra
   for brushing
2 tbsp. mirin
2 tbsp. chopped basil
2 tbsp. lemon juice

1 tsp. grated lemon zest
16 large scallops, cleaned
   and trimmed

**1** Preheat the oven to 400°F. Cut out four 14in. squares
of foil or baking parchment and brush lightly with oil.
**2** Put the oil, mirin, basil, lemon juice, and zest in a bowl
and mix well.
**3** Put 4 scallops in the middle of each piece of foil. Drizzle
the dressing over the top and gather up the foil to form
a sealed package. Put the foil packages on a baking sheet
and bake 10 minutes, or until the scallops are cooked
through when you open one package and test. Open the
packages and serve.

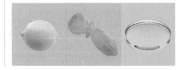

# spaghetti with chili mussels

The Thai seasonings in this pasta dish burst with flavor. Mussels are the perfect low-fat fast food, containing plenty of heart-protecting folic acid and B vitamins, as well as immune-boosting iron and zinc.

2 tbsp. olive oil
3 garlic cloves, crushed
2 tsp. grated gingerroot
2 red chilies, seeded and finely chopped
12 cherry tomatoes, halved

2lb. mussels in their shells, cleaned
½ cup dry white wine
12oz. spaghetti
1 handful basil, chopped

**1** Discard any open mussels that don't close when tapped. Heat the oil in a skillet over medium heat. Add the garlic, ginger, and chilies and cook 1 minute. Add the tomatoes, mussels, and wine, then cover the pan, and steam 3 to 4 minutes, shaking the pan, until the mussels open. Discard any that don't open.

**2** Cook the spaghetti in a large pan of boiling water for about 8 minutes, or according to the package directions, until al dente. Drain well and add it to the mussels. Toss gently to mix, sprinkle with the basil, and serve.

**SERVES 4**

**PREPARATION + COOKING**
15 + 15 minutes

**STORAGE**
Best eaten immediately, but leftovers will keep in the flavor until the following day.

**SERVE THIS WITH...**
Summer Greens with Mango Vinaigrette (see page 66)
Tropical Fruit Skewers (see page 139)

**HEALTH BENEFITS**
Ginger and chilies are wonderful circulation boosters and can help detoxify the body. Ginger also contains aromatic oils that have potent antiseptic properties and can help prevent nausea. Garlic is a powerful antioxidant, with volatile oils that can boost heart health and immune function.

# seafood stir-fry

This version of a favorite Chinese carry-out is also great with chicken, fish, or vegetables.

**SERVES 4**

**PREPARATION + COOKING**
15 + 6 minutes

**STORAGE**
Best eaten immediately, but leftovers will keep in the refrigerator until the following day.

**SERVE THIS WITH...**
egg or soba noodles
Chili & Sesame Broccoli
(see page 70)
Rose Water Rice Pudding with
Strawberries (see page 128)

**HEALTH BENEFITS**
Seafood is packed with protein, essential for the growth and maintenance of muscle and body tissues. It also supplies plenty of B vitamins, needed for healthy nerve tissue and energy production, plus the minerals iodine, zinc, and selenium.

1lb. 5oz. prepared seafood,
    such as shrimp, scallops,
    and squid rings
4 scallions, chopped
1 red bell pepper, seeded and
    sliced
1 garlic clove, crushed
8oz. canned pineapple pieces
    in juice, drained with juice
    reserved
1 tbsp. olive oil

Sweet & Sour Sauce:
2 tsp. cornstarch
2 tbsp. rice vinegar
½in. piece gingerroot, peeled
    and grated
1 tbsp. light brown sugar
2 tbsp. tomato ketchup,
    no added salt or sugar
1 tbsp. tamari

**1** Put the seafood, scallions, pepper, and garlic in a bowl and mix well.

**2** To make the sauce, blend together the cornstarch and vinegar. Put in a saucepan with the ginger, sugar, ketchup, tamari, and reserved pineapple juice and bring to a boil. Reduce the heat and simmer over low heat 5 minutes, or until thick.

**3** Heat the oil in a wok. Add the seafood and vegetables and stir-fry 3 to 4 minutes until cooked. Add the pineapple pieces and sauce to the wok and cook, stirring, 1 to 2 minutes until heated through, then serve.

# thai crab cakes

Many commercial fishcakes contain salt for flavoring and as a preservative. Using lime and wasabi paste (fiery Japanese horseradish) in these crab cakes makes them naturally flavorful without added salt.

10oz. white crabmeat
2 scallions, finely chopped
1 tsp. wasabi paste
1 tsp. tamari
¼ tsp. cayenne pepper

1 handful cilantro leaves,
  chopped
2 tsp. lime juice
2 tbsp. gluten-free flour
1 tbsp. olive oil

**1** Put all the ingredients, except the oil, in a food processor and blend until the mixture forms a coarse paste. Put the paste in a bowl, cover, and chill 15 minutes.
**2** Using your hands, shape the mixture into 8 equal-size patties. Heat the oil in a skillet until hot. Fry the crab cakes 3 to 4 minutes on each side until golden brown and cooked through. Serve hot.

**MAKES 8 CAKES**

**PREPARATION + COOKING**
15 + 15 minutes + chilling

**STORAGE**
Make in advance and keep, uncooked, in the refrigerator up to 2 days or freeze up to 1 month.

**SERVE THIS WITH...**
Asian Coleslaw (see page 67)
Garlic & Chili Sauce
  (see page 51)
Spice-Poached Pears
  (see page 135)

**HEALTH BENEFITS**
Crab is an excellent source of protein and of many heart-protecting vitamins, including folic acid and vitamin B6, and the minerals selenium, magnesium, potassium, and zinc. It also contains omega-3 fatty acids.

**SERVES 4**

**PREPARATION + COOKING**
10 + 15 minutes

**STORAGE**
Marinate the fish in advance
and keep in the refrigerator
up to 1 day.

**SERVE THIS WITH...**
Coconut Rice (see page 73)
Asian Coleslaw (see page 67)
Baked Pear & Spice Puddings
  (see page 129)

**HEALTH BENEFITS**
Citrus fruit contains a wealth of
plant chemicals and antioxidant
flavonoids that promote a
healthy immune system, reduce
inflammation, fight cancer, and
help prevent cardiovascular
disease. It is also rich in fiber,
making it excellent for the
digestive system.

# steamed snapper

Steaming is one of the best ways of retaining
all the flavor and nutrients in food, especially
for delicate fish.

2 red snapper, about 1lb. 2oz.
  each, cleaned
juice and grated zest of
  1 lemon
juice and grated zest of
  1 orange

¾in. piece gingerroot, peeled
  and grated
1 small red chili, seeded and
  chopped
2 scallions, chopped
1 handful cilantro leaves

**1** Make 5 or 6 diagonal slashes on each side of the fish.
Put them on a heatproof plate that will fit into a steamer,
or put each one on a large square of foil.
**2** Put the lemon and orange juices and zests, ginger, chili,
scallions, and cilantro in a bowl and mix well. Pour this
over the fish. Seal the foil packages, if using.
**3** Steam 15 minutes, or until the fish is cooked through.
Transfer the fish to plates and drizzle with the cooking
juices, then serve.

# thai fish balls in coconut

The fragrant herbs and spices in this dish provide loads of flavor without added salt.

1lb. 7oz. firm white fish fillets, such as coley, cod, or haddock
2 garlic cloves, crushed
2 tbsp. cornstarch
1 handful cilantro leaves, chopped
1 tsp. lemon juice

Coconut Sauce:
2 shallots, chopped
2 red chilies, seeded and chopped
2 garlic cloves
1 tbsp. olive oil
3 tomatoes, seeded and chopped
1¾ cups coconut milk

**1** Put the fish, garlic, cornstarch, cilantro leaves, and lemon juice in a food processor and blend 2 to 3 minutes until the mixture forms a paste. Using your hands, shape the mixture into 8 equal-size balls.
**2** Put the shallots, chilies, and garlic in a food processor and blend until the mixture forms a paste. Heat the oil in a large skillet. Add the paste and cook 1 minute.
**3** Add the tomatoes, coconut milk, and fish balls. Bring to a boil, then reduce the heat and simmer 5 to 7 minutes, turning the fish balls occasionally, until the fish is cooked and the sauce is thick. Serve immediately.

**SERVES 4**

**PREPARATION + COOKING**
15 + 8 minutes

**STORAGE**
Make in advance and keep, uncooked, in the refrigerator up to 1 day or freeze up to 1 month.

**SERVE THIS WITH...**
Spiced Flatbreads (see page 82)
Chili & Sesame Broccoli (see page 70)
Pomegranate-Orange Sorbet (see page 136)

**HEALTH BENEFITS**
White fish, such as coley, is a great source of protein and is also low in fat. The garlic, chilies, and shallots are potent immune boosters and fantastic foods for the heart—reducing "bad" cholesterol and high blood pressure and making the blood less sticky.

067

**HEALTH BENEFITS**
Salmon contains a chemical called dimethylaminoethanol or DMAE, an antioxidant that stimulates nerve function and protects cells from free-radical damage. It is also an excellent source of omega-3 fats, renowned for reducing the risk of heart disease and supporting the cardiovascular system.

# *seared salmon with gremolata

Gremolata, an Italian mixture of parsley, lemon zest, and garlic, has a punchy flavor without adding salt. Quick to make and full of vital immune-boosting antioxidants, it can also be stirred into pasta and rice dishes or drizzled over seared beef or lamb. The salmon in this recipe is an excellent source of omega-3 fats.

1 large handful flat-leaf
   parsley, finely chopped
juice and grated zest of
   1 lemon
2 garlic cloves, crushed
3 tbsp. olive oil

4 salmon fillets, skin on
10 red cherry tomatoes, halved
10 yellow cherry tomatoes,
   halved
freshly ground black pepper

SERVES 4

PREPARATION + COOKING
10 + 8 minutes

STORAGE
Prepare the gremolata in
advance and keep in the
refrigerator up to 3 days.

SERVE THIS WITH…
steamed green beans
or watercress salad
Lemon-Berry Cheesecake
 (see page 130)

**1** Put the parsley, lemon juice and zest, garlic, and 2 tbsp. of the oil in a bowl. Mix well.

**2** Pour the remaining 1 tbsp. oil over the salmon fillets and season with black pepper. Heat a skillet until hot. Sear the salmon, skin-side down, 2 to 3 minutes until golden. Turn the salmon over and cook 4 to 5 minutes longer until cooked through.

**3** Put the tomatoes in a bowl, add about 1 tbsp. of the gremolata, and toss well to coat. Spoon the tomatoes onto four serving plates and top with the salmon. Drizzle the remaining gremolata over the salmon and serve.

The anti-
inflammatory
components in parsley
and basil can ease
arthritis and bowel
inflammation.

# broiled sesame trout

**PREPARATION + COOKING**
5 + 8 minutes

**STORAGE**
Prepare the fish in advance and keep in the refrigerator overnight until ready to cook.

**SERVE THIS WITH…**
Mint & Lemon Zucchini
(see page 69)
Orange-Honey Sweet Potatoes
(see page 71)
Cherry & Ricotta Tarts
(see page 132)

**HEALTH BENEFITS**
Trout is rich in omega-3 fatty acids, important for healthy skin, joints, and heart. Sesame oil and seeds are high in omega-6 fatty acids and vitamin E for healthy skin and circulation, plus B vitamins to help the body cope with stress.

This speedy, nutrient-rich meal contains a wealth of health-promoting vitamins, minerals, and essential fatty acids. The sesame seeds add a wonderful crunchy texture to the dish and contain a compound called sesamin that helps protect the heart and liver.

4 trout fillets, about 7oz .each,
   skin on
4½ tsp. sesame oil

¼ cup sesame seeds
freshly ground black pepper

**1** Preheat the broiler to high. Brush the trout with about 1 tbsp. of the sesame oil and season with black pepper. Press the seeds onto the top and sides of the fillets.
**2** Heat a skillet over high heat. Add the trout, skin-side down, and cook 3 to 4 minutes until the skin is crisp.
**3** Transfer the trout, skin-side down, to a baking sheet and drizzle with the remaining oil. Broil 3 to 4 minutes until golden and cooked through, then serve.

# griddled tuna with mango & wasabi salsa

Wasabi, Japanese horseradish, is a great way to add vibrant flavor without adding salt.

5 tbsp. olive oil
juice of 1 lime
1 garlic clove, crushed
4 tuna steaks, about ¾ in. thick

Mango & Wasabi Salsa:
2 tbsp. lime juice
¼ tsp. wasabi paste
1 mango, peeled, seeded, and chopped
2 scallions, chopped
1 tomato, seeded and finely chopped
1 handful cilantro leaves, chopped

**1** Put the oil, lime juice, and garlic in a bowl. Mix well, add the tuna steaks, and let marinate 30 minutes.
**2** To make the salsa, put the lime juice and wasabi in a bowl, mix until blended, and then stir in the remaining ingredients; set aside.
**3** Heat a griddle pan until hot. Add the tuna steaks and cook 2 to 3 minutes on each side until cooked through. Serve with the salsa.

SERVES 4

PREPARATION + COOKING
15 + 6 minutes + marinating

STORAGE
Leftover tuna steaks can be kept in the refrigerator up to 2 days. Serve them cold in pita breads or add them to salads.

SERVE THIS WITH...
Asian Coleslaw (see page 67)
Spiced Flatbreads (see page 82)
Pomegranate-Orange Sorbet (see page 136)

HEALTH BENEFITS
Fresh tuna is an excellent source of omega-3 fats known as DHA (docosahexaenoic acid) and EPA (eicosapentaenoic acid). They are vital for brain function and a healthy nervous system and can boost our mood. Fresh tuna is a better choice than canned as the canning process destroys the omega-3 fats.

070

**SERVES 4**

**PREPARATION + COOKING**
10 + 25 minutes + marinating

**STORAGE**
Marinate the chicken in the
refrigerator the night before
to let the flavors develop.

**SERVE THIS WITH...**
Fruity Quinoa Salad
 (see page 62)
green salad
Rose Water Rice Pudding with
 Strawberries (see page 128)

**HEALTH BENEFITS**
Spices, such as cumin, chili,
and cilantro, are great digestive
aids and are a traditional Asian
remedy for gastrointestinal
disorders. They also possess
antimicrobial and antibacterial
properties, useful for fighting
coughs and colds.

# chermoula-spiced chicken

The spicy marinade known as chermoula uses
herbs and spices, rather than salt, for flavor.

1 tsp. ground cumin
1 tsp. ground coriander
1 handful cilantro leaves,
 chopped
1 handful parsley, chopped
1 red chili, seeded and
 chopped

1 garlic clove, crushed
juice and grated zest of
 1 lemon
½ tsp. paprika
4 boneless, skinless chicken
 breast halves
1 tbsp. olive oil

**1** Put all the ingredients, except the chicken and oil, in
a bowl and mix well. Rub the mixture all over the chicken
breasts. Cover and chill 2 to 3 hours, or overnight.
**2** Preheat the oven to 350ºF. Put the chicken in a roasting
pan and drizzle with the oil. Bake 20 to 25 minutes until
cooked through and the juices run clear, then serve.

# pesto-crusted chicken

Roasting the chicken with this delicious pesto keeps the meat moist and succulent. Chicken provides plenty of B vitamins, which are needed to make energy and respond to stress.

1 recipe quantity Pumpkin Seed
  Pesto (see page 48)
4 chicken breast halves,
  skin on

1 tbsp. olive oil
juice of 1 lemon

**1** Preheat the oven to 400°F. Ease the skin away from the chicken, leaving it intact on one side. Spread the top of each breast with the pesto and pat the skin back over to seal.

**2** Heat 1 tsp. of the oil in a skillet. Add the chicken, skin-side down, and sear 1 to 2 minutes until golden.

**3** Transfer the chicken to a roasting pan and drizzle with the lemon juice and remaining oil. Bake 20 to 30 minutes until cooked through and the juices run clear, then serve.

**SERVES 4**

**PREPARATION + COOKING**
15 + 35 minutes

**STORAGE**
Keep leftover chicken in the refrigerator up to 2 days.

**SERVE THIS WITH...**
Orange-Honey Sweet Potatoes
  (see page 71)
Balsamic-Roasted Beets
  (see page 68)
mixed salad
Chocolate & Orange Soufflés
  (see page 133)

**HEALTH BENEFITS**
Olive oil is a rich source of monounsaturated fat, which has a protective role in preventing heart disease and helps maintain levels of "good" cholesterol in the body. It is also less susceptible to damage from heat than sunflower and other seed oils.

**SERVES 4**

**PREPARATION + COOKING**
15 + 10 minutes + marinating

**STORAGE**
Leftovers can be kept in the refrigerator and used in wraps or pita breads the following day.

**SERVE THIS WITH...**
Coconut Rice (see page 73)
Asian Coleslaw (see page 67)
mixed salad
Pomegranate-Orange Sorbet
  (see page 136)

**HEALTH BENEFITS**
Yogurt is not only a great source of calcium for healthy bones and teeth, it also contains probiotic bacteria that might help to boost immunity, protect against infection, and support the digestive system. The calcium content is similar in low-fat and full-fat varieties.

# chicken tikka

Homemade curry sauces and pastes don't have to be complicated or time-consuming.

⅔ cup low-fat Greek yogurt
½ onion, finely chopped
1in. piece gingerroot, peeled
  and grated
1 garlic clove, crushed
1 tsp. ground coriander
2 tbsp. lemon juice

½ tsp. turmeric
1 tsp. garam masala
4 boneless, skinless chicken
  breast halves, cut into
  bite-size pieces
olive oil, for greasing

**1** Put all the ingredients, except the chicken and oil, in a bowl and mix well. Add the chicken, cover, and marinate in the refrigerator 2 to 3 hours.

**2** Soak eight bamboo skewers in water 30 minutes. Preheat the broiler to medium.

**3** Thread the chicken onto the skewers and put them on a greased baking sheet or broiler rack. Broil 7 to 9 minutes, turning halfway through, until lightly charred, cooked through, and the juices run clear, then serve.

# apricot-turkey burgers

These turkey burgers have a subtle sweetness, thanks to the addition of dried apricots.

¾ cup finely chopped dried
   apricots
2 tbsp. orange juice
1lb. ground turkey breast

2 shallots, finely chopped
2 tbsp. chopped parsley
2 tbsp. olive oil, plus extra
   for greasing

**1** Put the apricots and orange juice in a large bowl and let soak 5 minutes. Add the turkey, shallots, and parsley and mix well.

**2** Using wet hands, shape the mixture into 8 small patties or 4 large burgers. Cover and chill at least 30 minutes.

**3** Preheat the broiler to high. Put the burgers on a lightly greased baking sheet, then brush them with the oil. Broil 10 minutes on each side, or until cooked through. Alternatively, pan-fry the burgers 3 to 4 minutes on each side. Serve hot.

**SERVES 4**

**PREPARATION + COOKING**
15 + 20 minutes + chilling

**STORAGE**
Make in advance and keep, uncooked, in the refrigerator up to 2 days or freeze up to 1 month.

**SERVE THIS WITH...**
whole-wheat rolls
mixed salad
Orange-Honey Sweet Potatoes
  (see page 71)
Broiled Figs with Honey &
  Lemon Yogurt (see page 138)

**HEALTH BENEFITS**
Turkey is a nutritious, protein-rich food, low in saturated fat, and incredibly high in tryptophan, which is converted by the body into serotonin—the "feel-good hormone" that helps us sleep. Turkey is also a good source of the antioxidant selenium, important for a healthy immune system.

# roasted quail with pomegranate molasses

Pomegranate molasses adds a delightful sweet-sour taste to this dish.

**SERVES 4**

**PREPARATION + COOKING**
15 + 30 minutes + marinating

**STORAGE**
Leftover quail keeps in the refrigerator up to 2 days. Serve it cold with salad.

**SERVE THIS WITH...**
mixed salad
Fruity Quinoa Salad
  (see page 62)
Lemon-Berry Cheesecake
  (see page 130)

**HEALTH BENEFITS**
Poultry and game birds, such as chicken, quail, turkey, and duck, are good sources of stress-busting B vitamins, iron, zinc, and protein—important for immune health, tissue repair, and building new cells. B vitamins, especially folic acid, help lower levels of homocysteine, a high level of which is linked to heart disease.

**4 oven-ready quail**
**1 pomegranate, halved**

**Marinade:**
**¼ cup pomegranate molasses**
**2 garlic cloves, crushed**
**½ tsp. ground cinnamon**
**1 tbsp. olive oil**

**Dressing:**
**3 tbsp. pomegranate molasses**
**juice and grated zest of**
  **½ lemon**
**1 tsp. honey**
**3 tbsp. olive oil**

**1** Put all the marinade ingredients in a bowl and mix well. Pour it over the quail, cover, and chill 1 to 2 hours.
**2** Put all the dressing ingredients in a bowl and mix well.
**3** Preheat the oven to 400°F. Put the quail in a roasting pan and bake 30 minutes, turning once, until cooked through and the juices run clear. Remove from the oven and let rest 5 minutes.
**4** Hold the pomegranate over a bowl and bash with a wooden spoon to release the seeds. Slice the quail and arrange on four serving plates. Drizzle the dressing over the top, sprinkle with the pomegranate seeds, and serve.

# citrus seared duck

Fennel is rich in potassium, which can help regulate sodium levels in the body.

3 clementines
1 tbsp. fish sauce
juice of 1 lime
4 duck breast halves
1 tbsp. olive oil

1 fennel bulb, finely chopped
1 red onion, chopped
2 garlic cloves, chopped
freshly ground black pepper

**1** Preheat the oven to 400°F. Juice 2 of the clementines and segment the third. Put the juice and segments in a bowl and mix in the fish sauce and lime juice.
**2** Cut 5–6 diagonal slashes on the skin of the duck and season with black pepper. Heat a skillet over high heat until hot. Sear the duck 2 to 3 minutes on each side until golden, then reduce the heat and cook, skin-side down, 10 minutes. Transfer to a roasting pan and bake 10 minutes, or until cooked through and the juices run clear when pierced with a skewer or sharp knife.
**3** Heat the oil in the pan. Add the fennel, onion, and garlic and cook over medium-low heat 3 to 4 minutes until softened slightly. Add the clementine mixture and simmer 1 to 2 minutes until the sauce is bubbling and syrupy.
**4** Leave the duck to rest 5 minutes, then slice it. Spoon the vegetables and sauce over the top and serve.

**SERVES 4**

**PREPARATION + COOKING**
15 + 35 minutes

**STORAGE**
Make the clementine mixture in step 1 in advance and keep it in the refrigerator up to 3 hours. The cooked duck can be stored in the refrigerator up to 2 days.

**SERVE THIS WITH...**
Orange-Honey Sweet Potatoes (see page 71)
mixed salad
Cherry & Ricotta Tarts (see page 132)

**HEALTH BENEFITS**
Although duck is high in cholesterol, it is actually low in saturated fat, especially if the skin is removed. It is a good source of iron for a healthy immune system and of stress-busting vitamin B2. The citrus sauce provides plenty of immune-boosting vitamin C.

# marsala pork chops

Marsala, a fortified wine from Italy, has a sweet, robust flavor that makes it a perfect accompaniment to pork.

4 boneless pork chops
2 tbsp. all-purpose flour
2 tbsp. olive oil
4 sage leaves

1 tbsp. butter
2 garlic cloves, crushed
6 tbsp. Marsala
freshly ground black pepper

**1** Dust the pork with the flour and season with black pepper. Heat the oil in a skillet. Add the sage leaves and pork and cook the pork 6 to 8 minutes on each side until cooked through. Remove the chops from the pan and keep them warm.
**2** Add the butter, garlic, and Marsala to the pan. Heat 3 to 4 minutes until thickened.
**3** Spoon the Marsala sauce over the pork and serve.

# slow-roasted caribbean pork

Limes contain bioflavonoids, which, together with vitamin C, strengthen blood vessels and support the cardiovascular system.

2lb. 4oz. boned shoulder
  of pork, skin scored
1 red bell pepper, seeded
  and cut into chunks
½ pineapple, cored and cut
  into wedges
1 red chili, seeded and
  chopped

1 red onion, chopped
1 large handful cilantro leaves
juice and grated zest of 1 lime
1 garlic clove, chopped
¾ cup plus 2 tbsp. coconut
  cream
¼ tsp. ground cinnamon
2 tbsp. olive oil

**SERVES 4**

**PREPARATION + COOKING**
15 + 2 hours + marinating

**STORAGE**
Marinate the pork in advance
and refrigerate overnight.

**SERVE THIS WITH...**
Lemon-Paprika New Potatoes
  (see page 72)
mixed salad
Tropical Fruit Skewers
  (see page 139)

**HEALTH BENEFITS**
Coconut is a rich source of
lauric acid, which has antiviral
and antibacterial properties to
help the body fight infections.
Coconut oil is very stable and is
not damaged by heat, making it
an excellent choice for cooking.

**1** Preheat the oven to 350°F. Put the pork, pepper, and pineapple in a large roasting pan. Put the remaining ingredients in a food processor and blend 2 to 3 minutes until smooth. Pour the mixture over the pork. If time allows, cover and let marinate in the refrigerator at least 1 to 2 hours, or overnight.
**2** Cover the pan with foil and roast 2 hours, frequently spooning the juices over to baste. Remove from the oven and let rest 15 minutes. Slice and serve with the vegetables and pan juices spooned over the pork.

# vietnamese pork noodles

This Asian version of spaghetti Bolognese is low in salt, easy to make and a hit with kids.

SERVES 4

PREPARATION + COOKING
10 + 15 minutes

STORAGE
Leftovers keep in the refrigerator up to 2 days.

SERVE THIS WITH...
Asian Coleslaw (see page 67)
Spice-Poached Pears
  (see page 135)

HEALTH BENEFITS
Cucumber is a well-known diuretic—its high water and mineral content helps the body eliminate excess water and keep blood pressure down. A great detoxifier and rich in silica, it is a wonderful beauty food—great for healthy skin and hair.

1 tbsp. tamari
2 tbsp. sweet chili sauce
juice of 1 lime
1 tbsp. sesame oil
2 scallions, chopped

1lb. 2oz. ground pork
9oz. rice noodles
½ cucumber, cut into
  matchsticks
¼ cup plain yogurt

**1** Put the tamari, sweet chili sauce, lime juice, and 5 tbsp. water in a bowl and mix well.

**2** Heat the oil in a wok. Add the onions and pork and cook over medium heat 3 to 4 minutes, stirring occasionally, until brown. Add the tamari mixture and simmer 6 to 8 minutes until the meat is cooked through.

**3** Meanwhile, put the noodles in a heatproof bowl, cover with boiling water, and let stand 4 minutes, or according to the package directions, until tender. Drain well, add the noodles to the wok, and toss.

**4** Divide the pork and noodles into four serving bowls. Mix together the cucumber and yogurt, spoon it over the noodles, and serve immediately.

# polenta-crusted lamb

Rather than coating the lamb in bread crumbs, which can be high in salt, these chops have a lighter polenta crust flavored with fresh herbs. The coating works equally well on fish and chicken. Make this recipe gluten-free by using gluten-free flour.

8 boneless lamb chops
2 tbsp. all-purpose flour
1 egg, beaten
½ cup polenta or cornmeal

2 tsp. finely chopped thyme
2 tsp. finely chopped rosemary
2 garlic cloves, crushed

**1** Preheat the broiler to high. Flatten the lamb chops slightly with a rolling pin, then dust them with the flour.
**2** Put the egg in a shallow bowl. Mix together the polenta, herbs, and garlic and put the mixture on a plate. Dip the lamb in the egg, then coat with the polenta.
**3** Put the cutlets on a baking sheet and broil 5 minutes on each side until golden and cooked through, then serve.

**SERVES 4**

**PREPARATION + COOKING**
10 + 10 minutes

**STORAGE**
Make in advance and keep in the refrigerator up to 1 day.

**SERVE THIS WITH...**
Lemon-Paprika New Potatoes
(see page 72)
Mint & Lemon Zucchini
(see page 69)
Summer Berry Crisp
(see page 134)

**HEALTH BENEFITS**
Lamb, like other red meat, is a good source of iron and protein. It also provides plenty of B vitamins, especially B12, useful for boosting our mood as well as maintaining a healthy heart.

# lamb koftas with mint yogurt

These spicy koftas make wonderful finger food at barbecues.

2lb. ground lamb
2 onions, grated
2 garlic cloves, crushed
2 tsp. ground coriander
2 tsp. ground cumin
1 tsp. cayenne pepper
2 tbsp. chopped parsley
olive oil, for brushing

Mint & Yogurt Dressing:
$^2/_3$ cup plain yogurt
2 tbsp. chopped mint
freshly ground black pepper

**1** Put the lamb, onion, garlic, spices, and parsley in a large bowl. Mix well, cover, and chill 1 hour.
**2** To make the dressing, mix the yogurt and mint together in a bowl and season to taste with black pepper. Cover and chill until ready to serve.
**3** Soak ten bamboo skewers in water 30 minutes. Preheat a barbecue or broiler to high.
**4** Divide the lamb mixture into 10 equal pieces. Press each piece around a skewer to make a long sausage-shaped kofta. Brush with oil, then barbecue or broil the koftas 10 to 12 minutes, turning frequently, until golden brown and cooked through. Serve with the yogurt sauce.

# moroccan burgers

Serve these delicious burgers with a home-made tomato sauce, rather than salty, sugary, commercial ketchup.

1 red chili, seeded and
   chopped
1 large bunch cilantro
juice of ½ lemon
2 garlic cloves, crushed

1 tsp. paprika
½ red onion, finely chopped
1lb. 2oz. lean ground beef
olive oil, for greasing

**1** Put the chili, cilantro, lemon juice, garlic, and paprika in a food processor and blend 1 to 2 minutes until the mixture forms a paste. Put the onion and beef in a large bowl, add the chili paste, and mix well, using your hands.
**2** Shape the mixture into 8 burgers, then cover and chill 30 minutes.
**3** Preheat the broiler to high. Put the burgers on a lightly greased baking sheet and broil 7 to 8 minutes on each side until cooked through, then serve.

**MAKES 8/SERVES 4**

**PREPARATION + COOKING**
15 + 16 minutes + chilling

**STORAGE**
Prepare in advance and keep the uncooked burgers in the refrigerator up to 2 days or freeze up to 1 month.

**SERVE THIS WITH...**
Tomato Sauce (see page 19)
whole-wheat rolls
lettuce and sliced tomato
Chocolate & Orange Soufflés
  (see page 133)
fresh fruit

**HEALTH BENEFITS**
Tomatoes are rich in carotenoids, which are important antioxidants that can help slow down the aging process, reduce the risk of heart disease and stroke, and help guard the skin and eyes from sun damage. They're also high in lycopene—important for protecting against cancer, especially prostate cancer.

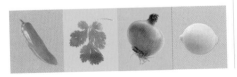

# pan-fried beef with raspberry dressing

Lean beef is an excellent source of iron and zinc, important for a healthy immune system.

**SERVES 4**

**PREPARATION + COOKING**
10 + 12 minutes + chilling

**STORAGE**
Marinate the beef in advance and keep in the refrigerator overnight.

**SERVE THIS WITH...**
leafy green salad
Fruity Quinoa Salad
(see page 62)
Baked Pear & Spice Puddings
(see page 129)

**HEALTH BENEFITS**
Walnuts are packed with essential omega-3 and omega-6 fatty acids, as well as monounsaturates, which are important for a healthy cardiovascular system. They lower LDL (or "bad") cholesterol and make the blood less likely to clot. They also contain ellagic acid, which has anticancer properties, as well as B vitamins for energy production.

1 tbsp. raspberry vinegar
2 tsp. crushed black
  peppercorns
2lb. sirloin steak
1/3 cup walnut pieces, toasted

Raspberry Dressing:
3 tbsp. raspberry vinegar
3 tbsp. walnut oil
3 tbsp. extra virgin olive oil
1 red onion, finely chopped

**1** Put the raspberry vinegar and peppercorns in a large shallow dish. Add the steak, and turn to coat, then let marinate 15 minutes.

**2** Put all the dressing ingredients in a bowl, whisk well, and set aside.

**3** Heat a skillet over high heat until hot. Add the steak and sear it 1 to 2 minutes on each side, then reduce the heat and cook 3 to 4 minutes longer on each side until the meat is cooked but still tender. Remove it from the pan and let rest 5 minutes.

**4** Slice the steak thinly and arrange on four serving plates. Sprinkle with the walnut pieces, spoon the dressing over the top, and serve immediately.

# steak with red wine sauce

This delicious red wine sauce is full of flavor without containing any salt.

4 sirloin steaks, about
   7oz. each
1 tbsp. olive oil
2 shallots, chopped

$^1/_3$ cup dry red wine
1 tbsp. red wine vinegar
1 tbsp. butter
freshly ground black pepper

**1** Season the steaks with black pepper. Heat the oil in a skillet, add the shallots and cook over medium heat 1 minute. Add the steaks and cook 4 to 5 minutes on each side until cooked but still tender. Transfer the steaks to a large plate. Let rest while you make the sauce.

**2** Add the wine, vinegar, and butter to the pan. When the butter melts, let the sauce simmer over low heat 1 to 2 minutes until thickened slightly.

**3** Slice the steaks and arrange them on four serving plates. Spoon the sauce over the top and serve.

**SERVES 4**

**PREPARATION + COOKING**
5 + 15 minutes

**STORAGE**
Best eaten immediately. Leftover steak will keep in the refrigerator up to 2 days and can be served cold in salads or sandwiches.

**SERVE THIS WITH...**
Lemon-Paprika New Potatoes
  (see page 72)
steamed green vegetables
Chocolate & Orange Soufflés
  (see page 133)

**HEALTH BENEFITS**
When drunk in moderation, red wine does have some health benefits. It contains the antioxidant resveratrol, which slows down the aging of the DNA in the body's cells. It helps control cholesterol levels and is thought to protect against heart disease and cancer.

**HEALTH BENEFITS**
Tofu is rich in phytoestrogens, hormonelike chemicals that might help reduce the risk of hormone-related cancers and symptoms of the menopause. It is also an excellent source of calcium and magnesium, important for healthy bones and teeth.

# sweet potato & coconut curry

Tofu, or soybean curd, is a complete protein, which means that it contains all of the essential dietary amino acids. Mild-tasting on its own, tofu takes on the vibrant flavors it is cooked with—so there's no need to add salt.

1 garlic clove, crushed
¾ in. piece gingerroot, peeled
  and grated
1 small onion, chopped
1 red chili, seeded and
  chopped
1 tbsp. lime juice
1 tbsp. olive oil
9oz. firm tofu, cut into cubes

2 tsp. turmeric
1 sweet potato, peeled and
  cut into cubes
1 red bell pepper, seeded
  and cut into chunks
5oz. green beans, cut in half
  crosswise
1²/₃ cups coconut milk
1 handful cilantro leaves

**SERVES 4**

**PREPARATION + COOKING**
15 + 30 minutes

**STORAGE**
Leftovers will keep in the
refrigerator up to 2 days.

**1** Put the garlic, ginger, onion, chili, and lime juice in
a food processor and blend until a paste forms.
**2** Heat the oil in a skillet. Add the tofu and fry over
medium heat, turning occasionally, 6 to 7 minutes until
crisp and golden. Remove from the pan with a slotted
spoon and drain on paper towels.
**3** Add the spice paste and turmeric to the oil in the
pan and cook 1 to 2 minutes until the mixture bubbles
gently. Add the sweet potato, pepper, beans, and coconut
milk. Bring to a boil, then reduce the heat and simmer
20 minutes, or until the potato is tender. Stir in the tofu,
sprinkle with the cilantro leaves, and serve.

**SERVE THIS WITH...**
Spiced Flatbreads (see page 82)
boiled rice
Spice-Poached Pears
 (see page 135)

**High-quality
proteins help fill
you up, stabilize
blood sugar levels,
and keep hunger
pangs at bay.**

# sun-dried tomato, red pepper & barley risotto

Adding barley to a risotto greatly increases the protein content and gives it a nutty flavor, so you don't miss the salt.

**SERVES 4**

**PREPARATION + COOKING**
15 minutes + 1 hour + soaking

**STORAGE**
Make in advance and keep in the refrigerator overnight. Reheat in the oven.

**SERVE THIS WITH...**
mixed salad
Cherry & Ricotta Tarts
(see page 132)

**HEALTH BENEFITS**
Barley provides plenty of insoluble and soluble fiber, selenium, and copper, as well as other minerals important for health. A rich source of beta-glucan, a fiber-type complex sugar, it can help lower cholesterol levels and support the immune system.

heaped ¾ cup pearl barley, soaked overnight
1 tbsp. olive oil
1 onion, chopped
2 garlic cloves, crushed
heaped ¾ cup arborio rice
5 sun-dried tomatoes in oil, drained and chopped
1 recipe quantity Roasted Peppers (see page 19)
4 tomatoes, peeled and chopped
2½ cups Homemade Vegetable Stock (see page 18)
2 tbsp. chopped parsley
¼ cup freshly grated Parmesan cheese or low-salt cheese

**1** Bring a large pan of water to a boil. Add the barley, cover, and cook, simmering, 35 minutes. Drain well.
**2** Heat the oil in a pan. Add the onion and garlic and fry gently 2 to 3 minutes until soft. Add the barley and all the remaining ingredients, except the parsley and cheese.
**3** Bring to a boil, then reduce the heat and simmer gently 20 minutes, stirring occasionally, until the rice is tender. Sprinkle with the parsley and cheese and then serve immediately.

# falafels with tahini sauce

This excellent protein-rich meal is a healthy vegetarian alternative to burgers.

15oz. canned chickpeas, no
    added salt or sugar, drained
    and rinsed
1 onion, chopped
1 garlic clove, crushed
1 tsp. cumin seeds
1 tsp. coriander seeds
2 tbsp. chopped parsley

2 tbsp. rice flour, plus extra
    for dusting
1 tbsp. lemon juice
1 tbsp. olive oil, for frying

Tahini Sauce:
juice of ½ lemon
2 tbsp. tahini
2 tsp. tamari

**1** To make the sauce, put the lemon juice, tahini, tamari, and 3 tbsp. water in a bowl and mix well, then set aside.
**2** To make the falafels, put the chickpeas, onion, garlic, seeds, parsley, rice flour, and lemon juice in a food processor. Pulse briefly until the mixture comes together.
**3** Shape the mixture into 8 small patties. Dust them lightly with the rice flour.
**4** Heat the olive oil in a skillet. Add the falafels, working in batches, if necessary, and fry 2 to 3 minutes on each side until golden brown. Serve the falafels warm with the tahini sauce for dipping.

**SERVES 4**

**PREPARATION + COOKING**
15 + 15 minutes

**STORAGE**
Make in advance and keep the uncooked patties in the refrigerator up to 2 days or freeze up to 1 month. The cooked patties will keep in the refrigerator up to 4 days. The sauce will keep in the refrigerator up to 1 week.

**SERVE THIS WITH...**
whole-wheat pita bread or
Spiced Flatbreads (see page 82)
mixed salad
Spice-Poached Pears
  (see page 135)

**HEALTH BENEFITS**
Chickpeas, lentils, mung beans, and adzuki beans are full of phytoestrogens called isoflavones, which help reduce menopausal symptoms, such as hot flashes and night sweats. Tahini is an excellent source of calcium and omega-6 fat.

# stuffed eggplant

This fabulous stuffed-vegetable dish is easy to prepare ahead of time—perfect for busy days.

**SERVES 4**

**PREPARATION + COOKING**
15 + 40 minutes

**STORAGE**
Make in advance and keep in the refrigerator up to 3 days.

**SERVE THIS WITH...**
Mint & Yogurt Dressing
 (see page 114)
Summer Greens with Mango
 Vinaigrette (see page 66)
Apple Crunch Cake (see page 85)

**HEALTH BENEFITS**
Pine nuts are an excellent source of protein and contain polyunsaturated fats that can help maintain low cholesterol levels. They are also rich in antioxidants, particularly vitamin E and zinc, important for healthy skin, heart, and immune system.

2 eggplants, halved lengthwise
1 tbsp. olive oil
¼ cup quinoa
½ tsp. ground cumin
⅔ cup Homemade Vegetable
 Stock (see page 18)
6 dried apricots, chopped
3 sun-dried tomatoes in olive
 oil, drained and chopped
1 tomato, chopped
1 tbsp. chopped mint
2 tbsp. pine nuts

**1** Preheat the oven to 400°F. Put the eggplants on a baking sheet, cut-side up. Brush with the oil, then bake 20 to 30 minutes until the flesh is lighy golden and tender.
**2** Meanwhile, put the quinoa, cumin, and stock in a pan. Bring to a boil, then reduce the heat and simmer slowly 15 to 20 minutes until cooked.
**3** Scoop out the eggplant flesh, leaving the skin intact. Chop the flesh and stir it into the quinoa with the apricots, tomatoes, mint, and pine nuts. Spoon the mixture into the eggplant shells. Put them back on the baking sheet and bake 10 minutes longer. Serve warm.

# roasted vegetables & dukkah

Dukkah, an Egyptian seasoning made with heart-healthy toasted nuts, seeds, and spices, is a great substitute for table salt.

1 red onion, quartered
2 zucchini, thickly sliced
1 small eggplant, cut into
    chunks
1 red bell pepper, seeded and
    cut into chunks
2 garlic cloves, crushed
4 plum tomatoes, quartered
olive oil, for drizzling

Dukkah:
4 tsp. sesame seeds
1 tsp. cumin seeds
1 tsp. coriander seeds
1 tsp. black mustard seeds
½ cup unsalted, shelled
    pistachio nuts

**1** Preheat the oven to 400°F. Put all the vegetables in a roasting pan, drizzle with olive oil, and roast 30 minutes until tender.
**2** To make the dukkah, put all the seeds and nuts in a skillet and toast lightly, stirring frequently, 1 to 2 minutes until the seeds start to pop. Transfer to a plate and let cool 2 to 3 minutes, then transfer to a food processor and pulse briefly until finely ground.
**3** Sprinkle the dukkah over the vegetables and serve.

**SERVES 4**

**PREPARATION + COOKING**
15 + 30 minutes

**STORAGE**
Make the dukkah in advance and store in an airtight container up to 3 days.

**SERVE THIS WITH...**
Lemon-Paprika New Potatoes
  (see page 72)
Cranberry & Date Balls
  (see page 91)

**HEALTH BENEFITS**
Pistachio nuts are rich in beneficial minerals, including calcium and magnesium for healthy bones. Together with the sesame seeds, they provide plenty of protein, essential fats, B vitamins, and vitamin E, important for heart health, brain function, and healthy nerve cells.

680

V ⊘

# vegetable tagine with dates & almonds

The vegetables, dates, and almonds in this Moroccan stew are full of healthy antioxidants.

**SERVES 4**

**PREPARATION + COOKING**
10 + 35 minutes

**STORAGE**
Make in advance and keep in the refrigerator up to 2 days or freeze up to 1 month.

**SERVE THIS WITH...**
couscous or quinoa
Spiced Flatbreads (see page 82)
Pomegranate-Orange Sorbet (see page 136)

**HEALTH BENEFITS**
Almonds are particularly high in vitamin E and zinc, which are important for skin health and can help prevent eczema, psoriasis, and dermatitis. Almonds also contain plenty of calcium, as well as monounsaturated fats and plant sterols, which can help reduce the risk of heart disease and lower cholesterol.

1 tbsp. olive oil
1 onion, chopped
3 garlic cloves, crushed
1 tbsp. garam masala
1 tsp. ground cinnamon
juice of ½ lemon
1 eggplant, cut into chunks
1 sweet potato, peeled and chopped

15oz. canned crushed tomatoes, no added salt
15oz. canned chickpeas, no added salt or sugar, drained and rinsed
²/₃ cup dried pitted dates, halved lengthwise
¹/₃ cup blanched almonds, toasted

**1** Heat the oil in a large Dutch oven. Add the onion, garlic, garam masala, and cinnamon and fry over medium heat 2 to 3 minutes, stirring occasionally, until soft.
**2** Add all the remaining ingredients and stir well. Bring to a boil, then reduce the heat and simmer, covered, 30 minutes until the vegetables are tender. Serve warm.

# lentil kedgeree & quail eggs

Brown basmati rice has a nutty flavor and keeps you feeling fuller longer. If you can't find quail eggs, use two hen eggs, quartered.

1 tbsp. olive oil
1 onion, chopped
2 garlic cloves, crushed
½ tsp. turmeric
10 cardamom pods, crushed
1 tsp. curry powder

1½ cups brown basmati rice
½ cup split red lentils
3 cups baby spinach leaves
8 quail eggs, hard-boiled, shelled, and halved
3 tbsp. chopped cilantro leaves

**1** Heat the oil in a pan. Add the onion, garlic, and spices and cook over medium heat 2 to 3 minutes until soft.
**2** Stir in the rice, lentils, and 3 cups water and bring to a boil, then reduce the heat and simmer, covered, 20 minutes until the rice is tender. Stir in the spinach. Serve immediately, topped with the eggs and cilantro.

**SERVES 4**

**PREPARATION + COOKING**
10 + 25 minutes

**STORAGE**
Leftovers will keep in the refrigerator up to 2 days.

**SERVE THIS WITH...**
Chili & Sesame Broccoli
  (see page 70)
Pomegranate-Orange Sorbet
  (see page 136)

**HEALTH BENEFITS**
Lentils are packed full of heart-protecting nutrients, including B vitamins, folic acid, selenium, magnesium, and potassium. Rich in iron and slow-releasing carbohydrates, they are great for boosting energy levels, too. Combined with the rice and quail eggs, the lentils provide plenty of protein.

# DESSERTS

Many processed and store-bought desserts contain startlingly high amounts of added salt. But that doesn't mean you have to avoid all your favorite treats. The homemade delicacies featured in this chapter all offer truly satisfying indulgence without compromising on taste. From rich, comforting Chocolate & Orange Soufflés to light and refreshing Tropical Fruit Skewers, there's something for everyone. The fruit-based desserts here are by far the best option if you want to cut down on salt—they're naturally high in potassium to help rid the body of excess sodium, reduce water retention, and lower high blood pressure. Best of all—they're delicious. Whatever you're in the mood for, you surely won't be disappointed.

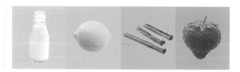

**SERVES 4**

**PREPARATION + COOKING**
10 + 40 minutes

**STORAGE**
Make in advance and keep in the refrigerator up to 2 days.

**SERVE THIS WITH…**
Chicken Tikka (see page 106)
Summer Greens with Mango
  Vinaigrette (see page 66)
Spiced Flatbreads (see page 82)

**HEALTH BENEFITS**
Strawberries contain plenty of vitamin C to help strengthen blood vessels and support the immune system, plus ellagic acid to protect body cells from free-radical damage. A great cleansing food, they are particularly useful for keeping the skin looking radiant and healthy.

# rose water rice pudding with berries

Using brown rice in this pudding provides more soluble fiber to keep you energized.

²/₃ cup brown basmati rice or
    arborio rice
3¾ cups milk
grated zest of 1 lemon
½ tsp. saffron strands

1 cinnamon stick
¼ cup fructose
2 tbsp. rose water
8 strawberries, hulled
    and sliced

**1** Put the rice in a saucepan and cover with plenty of water. Bring to a boil, then reduce the heat and simmer gently 15 minutes, or until the rice begins to soften.
**2** Drain well and return the rice to the pan. Add the milk, lemon zest, spices, and fructose. Bring to a boil, then reduce the heat and simmer, covered, 20 to 25 minutes, stirring occasionally, until the rice is tender.
**3** Stir in the rose water. Pour the rice pudding into bowls and scatter with the strawberries. Serve hot or cold.

# baked pear &
# spice puddings

This delicious pudding uses dried pears, which
are rich in heart-healthy potassium.

heaped 1 cup finely chopped
   dried pears
1 cup apple juice
1 piece candied ginger,
   chopped
1 tsp. apple pie spice
1 cup self-rising flour

½ tsp. baking soda
2 eggs, beaten
6 tbsp. olive oil, plus extra
   for greasing
6 tbsp. milk
plain yogurt or crème fraîche,
   to serve

**SERVES 4 OR 6**

**PREPARATION + COOKING**
15 + 30 minutes

**STORAGE**
Best eaten immediately.

**SERVE THIS WITH...**
Chermoula-Spiced Chicken
  (see page 104)
mixed salad
Lemon-Paprika New Potatoes
  (see page 72)

**HEALTH BENEFITS**
Pears are a useful source
of vitamin C, potassium,
and fiber, all important for
a healthy heart. They also
contain hydroxycinnamic acid,
a powerful antioxidant that helps
combat free-radical damage
associated with aging.

**1** Preheat the oven to 375ºF. Grease four or six individual
ovenproof or dariole molds, line them with baking
parchment, and put them on a baking sheet.
**2** Put the pears, apple juice, ginger, and apple pie spice
in a saucepan. Bring to a boil, then reduce the heat and
simmer 1 to 2 minutes until the juice becomes syrupy
and the pears soften. Set aside and let cool.
**3** Put the flour and baking soda in a bowl, then stir in
the eggs, oil, milk, and cool pear mixture to make a stiff
batter. Spoon the batter into the molds, cover with foil,
and bake 20 to 25 minutes until risen and golden. Serve
with yogurt or crème fraîche.

Ⓥ Ⓞ Ⓞ Ⓞ Ⓞ Ⓞ

# lemon-berry cheesecake

**HEALTH BENEFITS**
Ricotta cheese is an excellent source of calcium and is much lower in saturated fat and salt than many other cheeses.

This delicious cheesecake uses nutritious oats and almonds for a low-salt crust and features a light, luscious lemon filling. Lemons are a great source of bioflavonoids, such as rutin and quercetin, which work together with vitamin C to strengthen blood vessels, helping to prevent varicose veins and enhance circulation around the body.

4oz. unflavored, reduced-salt
  oatcakes, no added sugar
3 tbsp. finely ground blanched
  almonds
¼ cup (½ stick) butter, melted,
  plus extra for greasing
1 tsp. ground cinnamon

Filling:
2 eggs, beaten
¼ cup fructose
1lb. ricotta cheese, drained
3 tbsp. plain yogurt
3 tbsp. cornstarch
juice and grated zest of
  2 lemons
9oz. pure fruit blueberry
  preserve, no added sugar

SERVES 6 TO 8

PREPARATION + COOKING
15 + 50 minutes

STORAGE
Make in advance and keep in the
refrigerator up to 4 days.

SERVE THIS WITH...
Chicken & Artichoke Salad
  (see page 59)
Sun-Dried Tomato Bread
  (see page 80)

**1** Preheat the oven to 325ºF. In a food processor, blend
the oatcakes until fine crumbs form. Mix in the almonds,
butter, and cinnamon. Lightly grease an 8in. springform
pan. Press the mixture over the bottom of the pan, then
bake 15 minutes, or until light brown.

**2** Put all the filling ingredients, except the preserve, in
a blender. Process until smooth, pour over the crumb
crust, and bake 30 to 35 minutes. Let cool in the pan.

**3** Put the preserve in a pan and heat it over low heat
1 to 2 minutes until it softens slightly. Spread it over
the cheesecake and serve.

> **Use pure fruit
> spreads, rather than
> jam, as toppings for
> tarts and cakes to
> avoid unnecessary
> added sugars.**

# cherry & ricotta tarts

These easy tarts also make an ideal breakfast treat. Use canned cherries (in natural juice) when fresh ones are out of season.

28 cherries, pitted
1¼ cups ricotta cheese, drained
2 egg yolks

3 tbsp. finely ground blanched almonds
3 tbsp. Morello cherry pure fruit spread, no added sugar
olive oil, for greasing

**1** Preheat the oven to 350°F. Lightly grease four individual 4in. tart pans and put them on a baking sheet.
**2** Cut 12 of the cherries in half and chop the rest.
**3** Put the ricotta, egg yolks, almonds, and fruit spread in a blender and process until smooth. Stir in the chopped cherries and pour the mixture into the tart pans. Arrange the cherry halves on the top.
**4** Bake 25 to 30 minutes until set. Remove the tarts from the oven and let cool before serving.

**SERVES 4**

**PREPARATION + COOKING**
10 + 30 minutes

**STORAGE**
Make in advance and keep in the refrigerator up to 3 days.

**SERVE THIS WITH…**
Lemon Chicken & Asparagus Linguine (see page 65)
mixed salad

**HEALTH BENEFITS**
The cherry's deep red color comes from the powerful antioxidant compounds it contains. These support the immune system and protect against heart disease and cancer. They work together with vitamin C to help strengthen collagen, which is needed for healthy skin and blood vessels.

# chocolate & orange soufflés

This light, yet decadent, treat is full of anti-oxidants. It is hard to believe that something so delicious can actually be good for you.

3½oz. dark chocolate, at least 70 percent cocoa solids, chopped
juice and grated zest of 2 oranges
⅔ cup finely ground blanched almonds
4 eggs, separated
olive oil, for greasing

**1** Preheat the oven to 400°F. Lightly grease six ramekins.
**2** Put the chocolate in a heatproof bowl set over a pan of gently simmering water, making sure the bottom of the bowl does not touch the water. Stir until melted, then let cool slightly.
**3** Stir the orange juice and zest, ground almonds, and egg yolks into the melted chocolate. In a separate bowl, beat the egg whites with an electric mixer until stiff. Gently fold the egg whites into the chocolate mixture, then spoon it into the ramekins.
**4** Put the ramekins on a baking sheet and bake 10 to 15 minutes until risen. Serve immediately.

**SERVES 6**

**PREPARATION + COOKING**
15 + 20 minutes

**STORAGE**
Best eaten immediately. The soufflé mixture can be frozen, uncooked, in the ramekins. Bake from frozen 20 to 35 minutes.

**SERVE THIS WITH...**
Pesto-Crusted Chicken (see page 105)
Mint & Lemon Zucchini (see page 69)
fresh fruit

**HEALTH BENEFITS**
Chocolate, particularly dark chocolate with a high percentage of cocoa solids, contains antioxidants called phenols, the same chemicals that are found in red wine, which can help protect against heart disease. It also contains phenylethylamine, which creates the feel-good factor in the brain.

960

**134** THE TOP 100 LOW-SALT RECIPES

# summer berry crisp

This delicious summery dessert is bursting with antioxidants from the wonderful array of fresh berries. Topped with a super-nutritious, high-fiber crumble mixture, it will boost digestion and keep your energy levels soaring.

**SERVES 6**

**PREPARATION + COOKING**
10 + 30 minutes

**STORAGE**
Prepare the crumble mixture in advance and store in the refrigerator up to 4 days. You can make and chill the dish several hours in advance, then bake just before serving.

**SERVE THIS WITH…**
Crab & Fennel Salad
(see page 58)
Sun-Dried Tomato Bread
(see page 80)

**HEALTH BENEFITS**
Berries, particularly blueberries, are at the top of the list when it comes to antioxidant activity. Especially good for the eyes, they help night vision and protect against macular degeneration and cataracts.

²/₃ cup rolled oats
6 tbsp. wheat germ
¼ cup chopped almonds
2 tbsp. olive oil
¼ cup sesame seeds
¼ cup hulled hemp seeds
2 tbsp. honey
4½ cups mixed fresh or frozen berries

**1** Preheat the oven to 400°F. Put the rolled oats, wheat germ, almonds, oil, seeds, and honey in a bowl and mix well.
**2** Put the berries in a large baking dish. Sprinkle the crumble mixture over the top and press down lightly.
**3** Bake 25 to 30 minutes until golden and bubbling. Serve hot.

# spice-poached pears

Poaching fruit is a wonderful way of enhancing its natural flavor and sweetness.

2 cups red grape juice
1 tbsp. honey
4 star anise

4 pears, peeled, with
stems intact

**1** Put the grape juice, honey, and star anise in a saucepan and bring the mixture to a boil. Reduce the heat and simmer gently 10 minutes until slightly thick.
**2** Add the pears and cook over low heat about 15 minutes until tender. Transfer the pears to a serving dish. Strain the poaching liquid into a bowl, then spoon it over the pears. Serve hot or cold.

**SERVES 4**

**PREPARATION + COOKING**
5 + 25 minutes

**STORAGE**
Make in advance and keep in the refrigerator up to 2 days.

**SERVE THIS WITH...**
Moroccan Burgers
 (see page 115)
mixed salad

**HEALTH BENEFITS**
Like red wine, red grape juice contains an antioxidant called resveratrol, which helps protect the body from the effects of aging. It is packed with anthocyanins, which help strengthen capillaries and improve circulation and heart health. Red grapes contain higher levels of anthocyanins than white ones.

**HEALTH BENEFITS**
Compared to other juices and teas, pomegranate juice contains one of the highest levels of antioxidants, including polyphenols, tannins, and anthocyanins—important for supporting the immune system and protecting the heart.

# pomegranate-orange sorbet

This beautiful rosy-pink sorbet is crammed full of disease-fighting antioxidants—particularly polyphenols, which are important for heart health, protecting the body against cancers and delaying the effects of aging. The sweet oranges and pomegranate juice in this sorbet contain plenty of potassium, which is important for regulating salt levels in the body. Serve this in elegant wine glasses for a perfect summer dessert.

1¾ cups pure pomegranate
juice, without sugar or
sweeteners
2¾ cup freshly squeezed
orange juice

finely grated zest of 2 oranges,
plus extra for sprinkling
5 tbsp. honey
1 pomegranate, halved
4 to 6 mint sprigs

SERVES 4 TO 6

PREPARATION + FREEZING
(ICE-CREAM MAKER)
5 + 30 minutes

STORAGE
Make in advance and freeze
up to 2 months.

SERVE THIS WITH...
Roasted Quail with Pomegranate
  Molasses (see page 108)
Fruity Quinoa Salad
  (see page 62)
Amaretto Biscotti (see page 90)

**1** Put the pomegranate juice, orange juice, zest, and honey in a bowl and mix well.

**2** Transfer the mixture to an ice-cream maker and process according to the manufacturer's directions until frozen. Spoon the sorbet into a freezerproof container and freeze until firm. Alternatively, pour the mixture into a shallow, freezerproof container and freeze until ice crystals start to form, then remove the mixture from the freezer and blend in a blender to break up the ice crystals. Return to the container and freeze until firm.

**3** Hold the pomegranate over a bowl and bash with a wooden spoon to release the seeds. Scoop the sorbet into glasses. Sprinkle with the pomegranate seeds, orange zest, and mint sprigs and serve immediately.

**Citrus fruit contains vitamin C and bioflavonoids —antioxidants that help strengthen the walls of veins and arteries.**

# broiled figs with honey & lemon yogurt

Broiling or barbecuing is a great way to prepare fruit and enhance its natural flavors.

**SERVES 4**

**PREPARATION + COOKING**
10 + 17 minutes

**STORAGE**
Make the honey and lemon yogurt in advance and store in the refrigerator up to 4 days.

**SERVE THIS WITH...**
Polenta-Crusted Lamb
  (see page 113)
Orange-Honey Sweet Potatoes
  (see page 71)
Mint & Lemon Zucchini
  (see page 69)

**HEALTH BENEFITS**
Fresh figs are super-nutritious. In addition to plenty of fiber and potassium, they also contain serotonin to help us relax. A low intake of potassium-rich foods, especially when coupled with excess sodium, can lead to hypertension.

8 figs
¼ cup honey
juice and grated zest of
  1 lemon

Honey & Lemon Yogurt:
1 cup Greek yogurt
1 tbsp. honey
1 tbsp. lemon juice
2 tsp. grated lemon zest

**1** Preheat the oven to 400°F. To make the honey and lemon yogurt, put all the ingredients in a bowl and mix well. Cover and chill until required.

**2** Stand the figs upright and cut them into quarters by making two vertical cuts through each one, but do not cut through, so the figs stay intact. Lay eight pieces of foil in a baking tray. Put a fig in the middle of each.

**3** Put the honey and lemon juice and zest in a saucepan and simmer over low heat 1 to 2 minutes until the mixture thickens into a syrup. Spoon it over the figs, then gather up the foil around the figs to form eight sealed parcels.

**4** Bake 15 minutes, or until the figs are soft. Divide the figs onto four serving plates, pour any syrup over, and serve with the yogurt.

# tropical fruit skewers

This exotic potassium-rich dessert is a fun way to get kids to try new flavors.

2 passion fruit
5 tbsp. light coconut milk
1 tsp. honey
1 banana

1 large mango, peeled and pitted
1 papaya, peeled and seeded
½ pineapple, cored
olive oil, for greasing

**1** Soak four bamboo skewers in water 30 minutes. Preheat the broiler to high. Scoop the passion fruit pulp and juice into a bowl, then add the coconut milk and honey and mix well.

**2** Cut the banana, mango, papaya, and pineapple into 8 chunks each. Thread the fruit, alternating varieties, onto the soaked skewers and brush them with some of the passion fruit cream.

**3** Put the skewers on a lightly greased baking sheet and broil 3 to 4 minutes, turning occasionally, until light brown. Serve immediately with the remaining passion fruit cream spooned over the tops.

**SERVES 4**

**PREPARATION + COOKING**
10 + 4 minutes

**STORAGE**
Make the passion fruit cream in advance and keep in the refrigerator up to 2 days.

**SERVE THIS WITH...**
Vietnamese Pork Noodles
  (see page 112)
Chili & Sesame Broccoli
  (see page 70)

**HEALTH BENEFITS**
Fruit is a great source of potassium, which is useful for controlling the balance of water in the body. Papayas and bananas are particularly rich in this mineral. Potassium is also required by the body's cells to respond to thyroxin, the hormone that controls our metabolic rate.

# menu plans

## wheat- & gluten-free 5-day menu

Using fresh wholesome ingredients will make it easy to ditch the salt, wheat, and gluten from your diet.

**Day 1**

Breakfast: Pineapple, Lime & Avocado
Smoothie (see page 23)
Lunch: Chicken Rice Paper Wraps
(see page 50)
Dinner: Chicken Tikka (see page 106)

**Day 2**

Breakfast: Lemon Buckwheat Blinis
(see page 32)
Lunch: Crab & Fennel Salad (see page 58)
Dinner: Steak with Red Wine Sauce
(see page 117)

**Day 3**

Breakfast: Millet Hot Cakes (see page 31)
Lunch: Pea & Lettuce Soup (see page 46)

Dinner: Vietnamese Pork Noodles
(see page 112)

**Day 4**

Breakfast: Cardamom & Fruit Compote
(see page 26) with yogurt
Lunch: Corn & Pepper Fritters
(see page 55), using gluten-free flour
Dinner: Baked Sesame Trout (see page 102)

**Day 5**

Breakfast: Baked Beans (see page 36) with
Mediterranean Tortilla (see page 37)
Lunch: Pan-Fried Salmon with Tomato
& Bean Salad (see page 56)
Dinner: Vegetable Tagine with Dates
& Almonds (see page 124)

# vegetarian 5-day menu

This menu is designed to provide all the nutrients you need when following a low-salt, vegetarian diet.

**Day 1**

Breakfast: Oat Muffins with Eggs & Spinach
(see page 34)
Lunch: Roasted Garlic & Tomato Soup
(see page 45)
Dinner: Stuffed Eggplants (see page 122)

**Day 2**

Breakfast: Vanilla & Spice Granola
(see page 27)
Lunch: Artichoke & Onion Tarts
(see page 53)
Dinner: Roasted Vegetables & Dukkah
(see page 123)

**Day 3**

Breakfast: Blueberry Pancakes (see page 38)

Lunch: Balsamic-Roasted Beets
(see page 68)
Dinner: Sun-dried Tomato, Red Pepper
& Barley Risotto (see page 120)

**Day 4**

Breakfast: Apple, Cinnamon & Raisin
Oatmeal (see page 30)
Lunch: Pea & Lettuce Soup (see page 46)
Dinner: Falafels with Tahini Sauce
(see page 121)

**Day 5**

Breakfast: Millet Hot Cakes (see page 31)
Lunch: Avocado & Tomato Bruschetta
(see page 52)
Dinner: Sweet Potato & Coconut Curry
(see page 118)

# vegan 5-day menu

This menu avoids any foods derived from animals, including meat, fish, poultry, eggs, dairy, and honey. Wherever necessary, use fortified soy-, rice, or oat milks, yogurts, and cheeses in place of dairy products, and use maple syrup or agave nectar instead of honey.

**Day 1**
Breakfast: Fruit & Seed Bread
   (see page 84), served with nut butter
Lunch: Roasted Red Pepper Hummus
   (see page 42)
Dinner: Vegetable Tagine with Dates
   & Almonds (see page 124)

**Day 2**
Breakfast: Cardamom & Fruit Compote
   (see page 26)
Lunch: Roasted Garlic & Tomato Soup
   (see page 45)
Dinner: Stuffed Eggplants (see page 122)

**Day 3**
Breakfast: Pineapple, Lime & Avocado
   Smoothie (see page 23)
Lunch: Fruity Quinoa Salad (see page 62)

Dinner: Falafels with Tahini Sauce
   (see page 121)

**Day 4**
Breakfast: Vanilla & Spice Granola
   (see page 27)
Lunch: Citrus, Bean Sprout & Avocado
   Salad (see page 63)
Dinner: Roasted Vegetables & Dukkah
   (see page 123)

**Day 5**
Breakfast: Millet Hot Cakes (see page 31)
Lunch: Pea & Lettuce Soup (see page 46)
Dinner: Sweet Potato & Coconut Curry
   (see page 118)

# nut-free 5-day menu

Allergies to nuts and seeds are becoming increasingly common and, because the symptoms can be life-threatening, it is essential to take every precaution to avoid contact with nuts and by-products. This menu avoids all types of nuts and seeds. When buying any product, always check the label make sure it is nut- and seed-free.

**Day 1**

Breakfast: Spicy Tomato Juice
(see page 24)
Lunch: Lemon Chicken & Asparagus
Linguine (see page 65)
Dinner: Seared Salmon with Gremolata
(see page 100)

**Day 2**

Breakfast: Blueberry Buttermilk Pancakes
(see page 33)
Lunch: Butternut Squash & Pear Soup
(see page 44)
Dinner: Lamb Koftas with Mint Yogurt
(see page 114)

**Day 3**

Breakfast: Apple, Cinnamon & Raisin
Oatmeal (see page 30)

Lunch: Asparagus & Herb Frittata
(see page 54)
Dinner: Seafood Stir-Fry (see page 96)

**Day 4**

Breakfast: Cardamom & Fruit Compote
(see page 26)
Lunch: Lime & Chili Turkey Burrito
(see page 49)
Dinner: Moroccan Burgers (see page 115)

**Day 5**

Breakfast: Baked Eggs with Harissa
(see page 38)
Lunch: Spicy Stir-Fried Shrimp
(see page 64)
Dinner: Chermoula-Spiced Chicken
(see page 104)

# INDEX